T0042767

THIS JOURNAL BELONGS TO:

_____

PURPOSE

EVERYONE HAS THEIR OWN UNIQUE SET OF TALENTS, INTERESTS, AND LIFE EXPERIENCES THAT BRING THEM JOY OR GIVE THEM A REASON TO GET UP IN THE MORNING. LEARNING TO RECOGNIZE WHAT TALENTS YOU HAVE AND WHAT YOU LOVE TO DO CAN SET YOU ON THE PATH OF FINDING YOUR PURPOSE AND LIVING YOUR BEST LIFE.

FINDING ONE'S PERSONAL PURPOSE IS ESSENTIAL FOR HAPPY, HEALTHY LIVING. It can provide you with stability and direction to sustain you through life's challenges and setbacks, and it can make you feel more connected to others, by using your gifts to do good in the world.

We often have preconceived ideas about our purpose in life—get married, have kids, earn a certain amount of money, or achieve a certain position in society. These types of achievements, however, often do not bring the kind of fulfillment that comes with finding your personal sense of purpose. Ideally, your purpose blends with your interests, brings you joy, and has an ongoing impact on the world, whether large or small.

Sometimes it can be hard to recognize the things we are good at or most passionate about because they have become ingrained in our everyday life and thinking. The following pages contain questions and exercises designed to help you start thinking about what skills and talents you have, what excites and inspires you most, what you are passionate about, and what your life's purpose might be.

DISCOVERING YOUR PURPOSE

DISCOVERING YOUR PURPOSE

WHAT I LOVED TO DO AS A CHILD:

I'M HAPPIEST / FEEL MOST ALIVE WHEN I'M DOING THIS:

I CAN DO THIS FOR HOURS ON END:

I'M PASSIONATE ABOUT:

DATE ___/___/___

I'M REALLY GOOD AT:

THINGS THAT OTHERS THINK I'M REALLY GOOD AT:

THE UNIQUE QUALITIES THAT I HAVE:

WHAT I LOVE MOST ABOUT MYSELF:

WHAT MAKES ME FEEL PROUD:

DISCOVERING YOUR PURPOSE

MY CORE VALUES:

REAL WORLD ISSUES THAT CONCERN ME:

DATE ___/___/___

HOW I CAN USE MY TALENTS TO SERVE HUMANITY:

A UNIQUE CHALLENGE I'VE HAD TO OVERCOME, AND HOW I CAN HELP OTHERS FROM WHAT I'VE LEARNED:

I'VE WASTED TIME/ ENERGY ON:

I'D LIKE TO SPEND MORE TIME ON:

PEOPLE THAT INSPIRE ME:

DISCOVERING YOUR PURPOSE

MY LIFE FEELS IDEAL WHEN I AM:

(Mark your top 5 responses when your list is complete.)

01 _____

02 _____

03 _____

04 _____

05 _____

06 _____

07 _____

08 _____

09 _____

10 _____

LIFE'S PURPOSE VISION STATEMENT

STEP 1: Use the following page to summarize what you have discovered so far about your purpose and to record your responses to the 5 purpose prompts below. These key takeaways serve to form the draft for your personal vision statement.

1. Your strengths and passion.
2. Your core principles and values.
3. Skills you have that can solve real-world issues.
4. The role you want to have and why.
5. Short and long-term goals you'd like to accomplish.

DATE ___/___/___

WHAT I'VE DISCOVERED ABOUT MY LIFE'S PURPOSE:

MY LIFE'S PURPOSE VISION STATEMENT:

90-DAY PURPOSE JOURNAL

Now that you have gained more clarity about your interests, skills, and passions, use the pages of this journal to start being mindful of living your life's purpose. Take your time. You don't have to completely overhaul your life all at once. Start living your purpose a bit more fully every day, and pay attention to the results you are producing, how you are feeling, and the contribution you are making to the world.

MORNING REFLECTION

DATE ___/___/___

MY PURPOSE OR INTENTION FOR TODAY:

GOALS ALIGNED WITH MY PURPOSE:

ACTION STEPS I CAN TAKE TODAY:

- ☐
- ☐
- ☐
- ☐
- ☐
- ☐

A SELF-CARE GOAL FOR TODAY:

A CHALLENGE I'M FACING:

SOMETHING I'M EXCITED ABOUT:

HOW I SPENT MY TIME TODAY:

- ☐ MY LIFE'S PASSION
- ☐ VOLUNTEERING
- ☐ ONLINE/SOCIAL MEDIA
- ☐ WORKING
- ☐ SELF-CARE
- ☐ DOWN TIME
- ☐ TIME WITH FRIENDS/FAMILY
- ☐ TIME OUTDOORS
- ☐ OTHER: _____

EVENING REFLECTION

HOW I'M FEELING:

THIS BROUGHT ME THE GREATEST JOY TODAY:

SOMETHING I DID TODAY THAT FELT MEANINGFUL:

WHAT I DID TODAY THAT ALIGNED WITH MY PURPOSE:

A NOTABLE RESULT FROM LIVING MY PURPOSE:

A SETBACK I FACED TODAY AND HOW I CAN LEARN OR GROW FROM THIS:

MORNING REFLECTION

DATE ___/___/___

MY PURPOSE OR INTENTION FOR TODAY:

GOALS ALIGNED WITH MY PURPOSE:

ACTION STEPS I CAN TAKE TODAY:

- ☐
- ☐
- ☐
- ☐
- ☐
- ☐

A SELF-CARE GOAL FOR TODAY:

A CHALLENGE I'M FACING:

SOMETHING I'M EXCITED ABOUT:

HOW I SPENT MY TIME TODAY:

- ☐ MY LIFE'S PASSION
- ☐ VOLUNTEERING
- ☐ ONLINE/SOCIAL MEDIA
- ☐ WORKING
- ☐ SELF-CARE
- ☐ DOWN TIME
- ☐ TIME WITH FRIENDS/FAMILY
- ☐ TIME OUTDOORS
- ☐ OTHER: _____

EVENING REFLECTION

HOW I'M FEELING:

THIS BROUGHT ME THE GREATEST JOY TODAY:

SOMETHING I DID TODAY THAT FELT MEANINGFUL:

WHAT I DID TODAY THAT ALIGNED WITH MY PURPOSE:

A NOTABLE RESULT FROM LIVING MY PURPOSE:

A SETBACK I FACED TODAY AND HOW I CAN LEARN OR GROW FROM THIS:

MORNING REFLECTION

DATE ___/___/___

MY PURPOSE OR INTENTION FOR TODAY:

GOALS ALIGNED WITH MY PURPOSE:

ACTION STEPS I CAN TAKE TODAY:

- ☐
- ☐
- ☐
- ☐
- ☐
- ☐

A SELF-CARE GOAL FOR TODAY:

A CHALLENGE I'M FACING:

SOMETHING I'M EXCITED ABOUT:

HOW I SPENT MY TIME TODAY:

- ☐ MY LIFE'S PASSION
- ☐ VOLUNTEERING
- ☐ ONLINE/SOCIAL MEDIA
- ☐ WORKING
- ☐ SELF-CARE
- ☐ DOWN TIME
- ☐ TIME WITH FRIENDS/FAMILY
- ☐ TIME OUTDOORS
- ☐ OTHER: _____

EVENING REFLECTION

HOW I'M FEELING:

THIS BROUGHT ME THE GREATEST JOY TODAY:

SOMETHING I DID TODAY THAT FELT MEANINGFUL:

WHAT I DID TODAY THAT ALIGNED WITH MY PURPOSE:

A NOTABLE RESULT FROM LIVING MY PURPOSE:

A SETBACK I FACED TODAY AND HOW I CAN LEARN OR GROW FROM THIS:

MORNING REFLECTION

DATE ___/___/___

MY PURPOSE OR INTENTION FOR TODAY:

GOALS ALIGNED WITH MY PURPOSE:

ACTION STEPS I CAN TAKE TODAY:

- ☐
- ☐
- ☐
- ☐
- ☐
- ☐

A SELF-CARE GOAL FOR TODAY:

A CHALLENGE I'M FACING:

SOMETHING I'M EXCITED ABOUT:

HOW I SPENT MY TIME TODAY:

- ☐ MY LIFE'S PASSION
- ☐ VOLUNTEERING
- ☐ ONLINE/SOCIAL MEDIA
- ☐ WORKING
- ☐ SELF-CARE
- ☐ DOWN TIME
- ☐ TIME WITH FRIENDS/FAMILY
- ☐ TIME OUTDOORS
- ☐ OTHER: _____

EVENING REFLECTION

HOW I'M FEELING:

THIS BROUGHT ME THE GREATEST JOY TODAY:

SOMETHING I DID TODAY THAT FELT MEANINGFUL:

WHAT I DID TODAY THAT ALIGNED WITH MY PURPOSE:

A NOTABLE RESULT FROM LIVING MY PURPOSE:

A SETBACK I FACED TODAY AND HOW I CAN LEARN OR GROW FROM THIS:

MORNING REFLECTION

DATE ___/___/___

MY PURPOSE OR INTENTION FOR TODAY:

GOALS ALIGNED WITH MY PURPOSE:

ACTION STEPS I CAN TAKE TODAY:

- ☐
- ☐
- ☐
- ☐
- ☐
- ☐

A SELF-CARE GOAL FOR TODAY:

A CHALLENGE I'M FACING:

SOMETHING I'M EXCITED ABOUT:

HOW I SPENT MY TIME TODAY:

- ☐ MY LIFE'S PASSION
- ☐ VOLUNTEERING
- ☐ ONLINE/SOCIAL MEDIA
- ☐ WORKING
- ☐ SELF-CARE
- ☐ DOWN TIME
- ☐ TIME WITH FRIENDS/FAMILY
- ☐ TIME OUTDOORS
- ☐ OTHER: _____

EVENING REFLECTION

HOW I'M FEELING:

THIS BROUGHT ME THE GREATEST JOY TODAY:

SOMETHING I DID TODAY THAT FELT MEANINGFUL:

WHAT I DID TODAY THAT ALIGNED WITH MY PURPOSE:

A NOTABLE RESULT FROM LIVING MY PURPOSE:

A SETBACK I FACED TODAY AND HOW I CAN LEARN OR GROW FROM THIS:

MORNING REFLECTION

DATE ___/___/___

MY PURPOSE OR INTENTION FOR TODAY:

GOALS ALIGNED WITH MY PURPOSE:

ACTION STEPS I CAN TAKE TODAY:

- ☐
- ☐
- ☐
- ☐
- ☐
- ☐

A SELF-CARE GOAL FOR TODAY:

A CHALLENGE I'M FACING:

SOMETHING I'M EXCITED ABOUT:

HOW I SPENT MY TIME TODAY:

- ☐ MY LIFE'S PASSION
- ☐ VOLUNTEERING
- ☐ ONLINE/SOCIAL MEDIA
- ☐ WORKING
- ☐ SELF-CARE
- ☐ DOWN TIME
- ☐ TIME WITH FRIENDS/FAMILY
- ☐ TIME OUTDOORS
- ☐ OTHER: _____

EVENING REFLECTION

HOW I'M FEELING:

THIS BROUGHT ME THE GREATEST JOY TODAY:

SOMETHING I DID TODAY THAT FELT MEANINGFUL:

WHAT I DID TODAY THAT ALIGNED WITH MY PURPOSE:

A NOTABLE RESULT FROM LIVING MY PURPOSE:

A SETBACK I FACED TODAY AND HOW I CAN LEARN OR GROW FROM THIS:

MORNING REFLECTION

DATE ___/___/___

MY PURPOSE OR INTENTION FOR TODAY:

GOALS ALIGNED WITH MY PURPOSE:

ACTION STEPS I CAN TAKE TODAY:

- ☐
- ☐
- ☐
- ☐
- ☐
- ☐

A SELF-CARE GOAL FOR TODAY:

A CHALLENGE I'M FACING:

SOMETHING I'M EXCITED ABOUT:

HOW I SPENT MY TIME TODAY:

- ☐ MY LIFE'S PASSION
- ☐ VOLUNTEERING
- ☐ ONLINE/SOCIAL MEDIA
- ☐ WORKING
- ☐ SELF-CARE
- ☐ DOWN TIME
- ☐ TIME WITH FRIENDS/FAMILY
- ☐ TIME OUTDOORS
- ☐ OTHER: _____

EVENING REFLECTION

HOW I'M FEELING:

THIS BROUGHT ME THE GREATEST JOY TODAY:

SOMETHING I DID TODAY THAT FELT MEANINGFUL:

WHAT I DID TODAY THAT ALIGNED WITH MY PURPOSE:

A NOTABLE RESULT FROM LIVING MY PURPOSE:

A SETBACK I FACED TODAY AND HOW I CAN LEARN OR GROW FROM THIS:

MORNING REFLECTION

DATE ___/___/___

MY PURPOSE OR INTENTION FOR TODAY:

GOALS ALIGNED WITH MY PURPOSE:

ACTION STEPS I CAN TAKE TODAY:

- ☐
- ☐
- ☐
- ☐
- ☐
- ☐

A SELF-CARE GOAL FOR TODAY:

A CHALLENGE I'M FACING:

SOMETHING I'M EXCITED ABOUT:

HOW I SPENT MY TIME TODAY:

- ☐ MY LIFE'S PASSION
- ☐ VOLUNTEERING
- ☐ ONLINE/SOCIAL MEDIA
- ☐ WORKING
- ☐ SELF-CARE
- ☐ DOWN TIME
- ☐ TIME WITH FRIENDS/FAMILY
- ☐ TIME OUTDOORS
- ☐ OTHER: _____

EVENING REFLECTION

HOW I'M FEELING:

THIS BROUGHT ME THE GREATEST JOY TODAY:

SOMETHING I DID TODAY THAT FELT MEANINGFUL:

WHAT I DID TODAY THAT ALIGNED WITH MY PURPOSE:

A NOTABLE RESULT FROM LIVING MY PURPOSE:

A SETBACK I FACED TODAY AND HOW I CAN LEARN OR GROW FROM THIS:

MORNING REFLECTION

DATE ___/___/___

MY PURPOSE OR INTENTION FOR TODAY:

GOALS ALIGNED WITH MY PURPOSE:

ACTION STEPS I CAN TAKE TODAY:

- ☐
- ☐
- ☐
- ☐
- ☐
- ☐

A SELF-CARE GOAL FOR TODAY:

A CHALLENGE I'M FACING:

SOMETHING I'M EXCITED ABOUT:

HOW I SPENT MY TIME TODAY:

- ☐ MY LIFE'S PASSION
- ☐ VOLUNTEERING
- ☐ ONLINE/SOCIAL MEDIA
- ☐ WORKING
- ☐ SELF-CARE
- ☐ DOWN TIME
- ☐ TIME WITH FRIENDS/FAMILY
- ☐ TIME OUTDOORS
- ☐ OTHER: _____

EVENING REFLECTION

HOW I'M FEELING:

THIS BROUGHT ME THE GREATEST JOY TODAY:

SOMETHING I DID TODAY THAT FELT MEANINGFUL:

WHAT I DID TODAY THAT ALIGNED WITH MY PURPOSE:

A NOTABLE RESULT FROM LIVING MY PURPOSE:

A SETBACK I FACED TODAY AND HOW I CAN LEARN OR GROW FROM THIS:

MORNING REFLECTION

DATE ___/___/___

MY PURPOSE OR INTENTION FOR TODAY:

GOALS ALIGNED WITH MY PURPOSE:

ACTION STEPS I CAN TAKE TODAY:

- ☐
- ☐
- ☐
- ☐
- ☐
- ☐

A SELF-CARE GOAL FOR TODAY:

A CHALLENGE I'M FACING:

SOMETHING I'M EXCITED ABOUT:

HOW I SPENT MY TIME TODAY:

- ☐ MY LIFE'S PASSION
- ☐ VOLUNTEERING
- ☐ ONLINE/SOCIAL MEDIA
- ☐ WORKING
- ☐ SELF-CARE
- ☐ DOWN TIME
- ☐ TIME WITH FRIENDS/FAMILY
- ☐ TIME OUTDOORS
- ☐ OTHER: _____

EVENING REFLECTION

HOW I'M FEELING:

THIS BROUGHT ME THE GREATEST JOY TODAY:

SOMETHING I DID TODAY THAT FELT MEANINGFUL:

WHAT I DID TODAY THAT ALIGNED WITH MY PURPOSE:

A NOTABLE RESULT FROM LIVING MY PURPOSE:

A SETBACK I FACED TODAY AND HOW I CAN LEARN OR GROW FROM THIS:

MORNING REFLECTION

DATE ___/___/___

MY PURPOSE OR INTENTION FOR TODAY:

GOALS ALIGNED WITH MY PURPOSE:

ACTION STEPS I CAN TAKE TODAY:

- ☐
- ☐
- ☐
- ☐
- ☐
- ☐

A SELF-CARE GOAL FOR TODAY:

A CHALLENGE I'M FACING:

SOMETHING I'M EXCITED ABOUT:

HOW I SPENT MY TIME TODAY:

- ☐ MY LIFE'S PASSION
- ☐ VOLUNTEERING
- ☐ ONLINE/SOCIAL MEDIA
- ☐ WORKING
- ☐ SELF-CARE
- ☐ DOWN TIME
- ☐ TIME WITH FRIENDS/FAMILY
- ☐ TIME OUTDOORS
- ☐ OTHER: _____

EVENING REFLECTION

HOW I'M FEELING:

THIS BROUGHT ME THE GREATEST JOY TODAY:

SOMETHING I DID TODAY THAT FELT MEANINGFUL:

WHAT I DID TODAY THAT ALIGNED WITH MY PURPOSE:

A NOTABLE RESULT FROM LIVING MY PURPOSE:

A SETBACK I FACED TODAY AND HOW I CAN LEARN OR GROW FROM THIS:

MORNING REFLECTION

DATE ___/___/___

MY PURPOSE OR INTENTION FOR TODAY:

GOALS ALIGNED WITH MY PURPOSE:

ACTION STEPS I CAN TAKE TODAY:

- ☐
- ☐
- ☐
- ☐
- ☐
- ☐

A SELF-CARE GOAL FOR TODAY:

A CHALLENGE I'M FACING:

SOMETHING I'M EXCITED ABOUT:

HOW I SPENT MY TIME TODAY:

- ☐ MY LIFE'S PASSION
- ☐ VOLUNTEERING
- ☐ ONLINE/SOCIAL MEDIA
- ☐ WORKING
- ☐ SELF-CARE
- ☐ DOWN TIME
- ☐ TIME WITH FRIENDS/FAMILY
- ☐ TIME OUTDOORS
- ☐ OTHER: _____

EVENING REFLECTION

HOW I'M FEELING:

THIS BROUGHT ME THE GREATEST JOY TODAY:

SOMETHING I DID TODAY THAT FELT MEANINGFUL:

WHAT I DID TODAY THAT ALIGNED WITH MY PURPOSE:

A NOTABLE RESULT FROM LIVING MY PURPOSE:

A SETBACK I FACED TODAY AND HOW I CAN LEARN OR GROW FROM THIS:

MORNING REFLECTION

DATE ___/___/___

MY PURPOSE OR INTENTION FOR TODAY:

GOALS ALIGNED WITH MY PURPOSE:

ACTION STEPS I CAN TAKE TODAY:

- ☐
- ☐
- ☐
- ☐
- ☐
- ☐

A SELF-CARE GOAL FOR TODAY:

A CHALLENGE I'M FACING:

SOMETHING I'M EXCITED ABOUT:

HOW I SPENT MY TIME TODAY:

- ☐ MY LIFE'S PASSION
- ☐ VOLUNTEERING
- ☐ ONLINE/SOCIAL MEDIA
- ☐ WORKING
- ☐ SELF-CARE
- ☐ DOWN TIME
- ☐ TIME WITH FRIENDS/FAMILY
- ☐ TIME OUTDOORS
- ☐ OTHER: _____

EVENING REFLECTION

HOW I'M FEELING:

THIS BROUGHT ME THE GREATEST JOY TODAY:

SOMETHING I DID TODAY THAT FELT MEANINGFUL:

WHAT I DID TODAY THAT ALIGNED WITH MY PURPOSE:

A NOTABLE RESULT FROM LIVING MY PURPOSE:

A SETBACK I FACED TODAY AND HOW I CAN LEARN OR GROW FROM THIS:

MORNING REFLECTION

DATE ___/___/___

MY PURPOSE OR INTENTION FOR TODAY:

GOALS ALIGNED WITH MY PURPOSE:

ACTION STEPS I CAN TAKE TODAY:

- ☐
- ☐
- ☐
- ☐
- ☐
- ☐

A SELF-CARE GOAL FOR TODAY:

A CHALLENGE I'M FACING:

SOMETHING I'M EXCITED ABOUT:

HOW I SPENT MY TIME TODAY:

- ☐ MY LIFE'S PASSION
- ☐ VOLUNTEERING
- ☐ ONLINE/SOCIAL MEDIA
- ☐ WORKING
- ☐ SELF-CARE
- ☐ DOWN TIME
- ☐ TIME WITH FRIENDS/FAMILY
- ☐ TIME OUTDOORS
- ☐ OTHER: _____

EVENING REFLECTION

HOW I'M FEELING:

THIS BROUGHT ME THE GREATEST JOY TODAY:

SOMETHING I DID TODAY THAT FELT MEANINGFUL:

WHAT I DID TODAY THAT ALIGNED WITH MY PURPOSE:

A NOTABLE RESULT FROM LIVING MY PURPOSE:

A SETBACK I FACED TODAY AND HOW I CAN LEARN OR GROW FROM THIS:

MORNING REFLECTION

DATE ___/___/___

MY PURPOSE OR INTENTION FOR TODAY:

GOALS ALIGNED WITH MY PURPOSE:

ACTION STEPS I CAN TAKE TODAY:

- ☐
- ☐
- ☐
- ☐
- ☐
- ☐

A SELF-CARE GOAL FOR TODAY:

A CHALLENGE I'M FACING:

SOMETHING I'M EXCITED ABOUT:

HOW I SPENT MY TIME TODAY:

- ☐ MY LIFE'S PASSION
- ☐ VOLUNTEERING
- ☐ ONLINE/SOCIAL MEDIA
- ☐ WORKING
- ☐ SELF-CARE
- ☐ DOWN TIME
- ☐ TIME WITH FRIENDS/FAMILY
- ☐ TIME OUTDOORS
- ☐ OTHER: _____

EVENING REFLECTION

HOW I'M FEELING:

THIS BROUGHT ME THE GREATEST JOY TODAY:

SOMETHING I DID TODAY THAT FELT MEANINGFUL:

WHAT I DID TODAY THAT ALIGNED WITH MY PURPOSE:

A NOTABLE RESULT FROM LIVING MY PURPOSE:

A SETBACK I FACED TODAY AND HOW I CAN LEARN OR GROW FROM THIS:

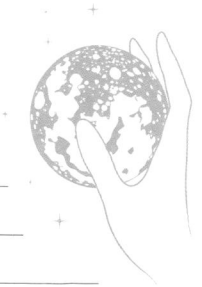

MORNING REFLECTION

DATE ___/___/___

MY PURPOSE OR INTENTION FOR TODAY:

GOALS ALIGNED WITH MY PURPOSE:

ACTION STEPS I CAN TAKE TODAY:

- ☐
- ☐
- ☐
- ☐
- ☐
- ☐

A SELF-CARE GOAL FOR TODAY:

A CHALLENGE I'M FACING:

SOMETHING I'M EXCITED ABOUT:

HOW I SPENT MY TIME TODAY:

- ☐ MY LIFE'S PASSION
- ☐ VOLUNTEERING
- ☐ ONLINE/SOCIAL MEDIA
- ☐ WORKING
- ☐ SELF-CARE
- ☐ DOWN TIME
- ☐ TIME WITH FRIENDS/FAMILY
- ☐ TIME OUTDOORS
- ☐ OTHER: _____

EVENING REFLECTION

HOW I'M FEELING:

THIS BROUGHT ME THE GREATEST JOY TODAY:

SOMETHING I DID TODAY THAT FELT MEANINGFUL:

WHAT I DID TODAY THAT ALIGNED WITH MY PURPOSE:

A NOTABLE RESULT FROM LIVING MY PURPOSE:

A SETBACK I FACED TODAY AND HOW I CAN LEARN OR GROW FROM THIS:

MORNING REFLECTION

DATE ___/___/___

MY PURPOSE OR INTENTION FOR TODAY:

GOALS ALIGNED WITH MY PURPOSE:

ACTION STEPS I CAN TAKE TODAY:

- ☐
- ☐
- ☐
- ☐
- ☐
- ☐

A SELF-CARE GOAL FOR TODAY:

A CHALLENGE I'M FACING:

SOMETHING I'M EXCITED ABOUT:

HOW I SPENT MY TIME TODAY:

- ☐ MY LIFE'S PASSION
- ☐ VOLUNTEERING
- ☐ ONLINE/SOCIAL MEDIA
- ☐ WORKING
- ☐ SELF-CARE
- ☐ DOWN TIME
- ☐ TIME WITH FRIENDS/FAMILY
- ☐ TIME OUTDOORS
- ☐ OTHER: _____

EVENING REFLECTION

HOW I'M FEELING:

THIS BROUGHT ME THE GREATEST JOY TODAY:

SOMETHING I DID TODAY THAT FELT MEANINGFUL:

WHAT I DID TODAY THAT ALIGNED WITH MY PURPOSE:

A NOTABLE RESULT FROM LIVING MY PURPOSE:

A SETBACK I FACED TODAY AND HOW I CAN LEARN OR GROW FROM THIS:

MORNING REFLECTION

DATE ___/___/___

MY PURPOSE OR INTENTION FOR TODAY:

GOALS ALIGNED WITH MY PURPOSE:

ACTION STEPS I CAN TAKE TODAY:

- ☐
- ☐
- ☐
- ☐
- ☐
- ☐

A SELF-CARE GOAL FOR TODAY:

A CHALLENGE I'M FACING:

SOMETHING I'M EXCITED ABOUT:

HOW I SPENT MY TIME TODAY:

- ☐ MY LIFE'S PASSION
- ☐ VOLUNTEERING
- ☐ ONLINE/SOCIAL MEDIA
- ☐ WORKING
- ☐ SELF-CARE
- ☐ DOWN TIME
- ☐ TIME WITH FRIENDS/FAMILY
- ☐ TIME OUTDOORS
- ☐ OTHER: _____

EVENING REFLECTION

HOW I'M FEELING:

THIS BROUGHT ME THE GREATEST JOY TODAY:

SOMETHING I DID TODAY THAT FELT MEANINGFUL:

WHAT I DID TODAY THAT ALIGNED WITH MY PURPOSE:

A NOTABLE RESULT FROM LIVING MY PURPOSE:

A SETBACK I FACED TODAY AND HOW I CAN LEARN OR GROW FROM THIS:

MORNING REFLECTION

DATE ___/___/___

MY PURPOSE OR INTENTION FOR TODAY:

GOALS ALIGNED WITH MY PURPOSE:

ACTION STEPS I CAN TAKE TODAY:

- ☐
- ☐
- ☐
- ☐
- ☐
- ☐

A SELF-CARE GOAL FOR TODAY:

A CHALLENGE I'M FACING:

SOMETHING I'M EXCITED ABOUT:

HOW I SPENT MY TIME TODAY:

- ☐ MY LIFE'S PASSION
- ☐ VOLUNTEERING
- ☐ ONLINE/SOCIAL MEDIA
- ☐ WORKING
- ☐ SELF-CARE
- ☐ DOWN TIME
- ☐ TIME WITH FRIENDS/FAMILY
- ☐ TIME OUTDOORS
- ☐ OTHER: _____

EVENING REFLECTION

HOW I'M FEELING:

THIS BROUGHT ME THE GREATEST JOY TODAY:

SOMETHING I DID TODAY THAT FELT MEANINGFUL:

WHAT I DID TODAY THAT ALIGNED WITH MY PURPOSE:

A NOTABLE RESULT FROM LIVING MY PURPOSE:

A SETBACK I FACED TODAY AND HOW I CAN LEARN OR GROW FROM THIS:

MORNING REFLECTION

DATE ___/___/___

MY PURPOSE OR INTENTION FOR TODAY:

GOALS ALIGNED WITH MY PURPOSE:

ACTION STEPS I CAN TAKE TODAY:

- ☐
- ☐
- ☐
- ☐
- ☐
- ☐

A SELF-CARE GOAL FOR TODAY:

A CHALLENGE I'M FACING:

SOMETHING I'M EXCITED ABOUT:

HOW I SPENT MY TIME TODAY:

- ☐ MY LIFE'S PASSION
- ☐ VOLUNTEERING
- ☐ ONLINE/SOCIAL MEDIA
- ☐ WORKING
- ☐ SELF-CARE
- ☐ DOWN TIME
- ☐ TIME WITH FRIENDS/FAMILY
- ☐ TIME OUTDOORS
- ☐ OTHER: _____

EVENING REFLECTION

HOW I'M FEELING:

THIS BROUGHT ME THE GREATEST JOY TODAY:

SOMETHING I DID TODAY THAT FELT MEANINGFUL:

WHAT I DID TODAY THAT ALIGNED WITH MY PURPOSE:

A NOTABLE RESULT FROM LIVING MY PURPOSE:

A SETBACK I FACED TODAY AND HOW I CAN LEARN OR GROW FROM THIS:

MORNING REFLECTION

DATE ___/___/___

MY PURPOSE OR INTENTION FOR TODAY:

GOALS ALIGNED WITH MY PURPOSE:

ACTION STEPS I CAN TAKE TODAY:

- ☐
- ☐
- ☐
- ☐
- ☐
- ☐

A SELF-CARE GOAL FOR TODAY:

A CHALLENGE I'M FACING:

SOMETHING I'M EXCITED ABOUT:

HOW I SPENT MY TIME TODAY:

- ☐ MY LIFE'S PASSION
- ☐ VOLUNTEERING
- ☐ ONLINE/SOCIAL MEDIA
- ☐ WORKING
- ☐ SELF-CARE
- ☐ DOWN TIME
- ☐ TIME WITH FRIENDS/FAMILY
- ☐ TIME OUTDOORS
- ☐ OTHER: _____

EVENING REFLECTION

HOW I'M FEELING:

THIS BROUGHT ME THE GREATEST JOY TODAY:

SOMETHING I DID TODAY THAT FELT MEANINGFUL:

WHAT I DID TODAY THAT ALIGNED WITH MY PURPOSE:

A NOTABLE RESULT FROM LIVING MY PURPOSE:

A SETBACK I FACED TODAY AND HOW I CAN LEARN OR GROW FROM THIS:

MORNING REFLECTION

DATE ___/___/___

MY PURPOSE OR INTENTION FOR TODAY:

GOALS ALIGNED WITH MY PURPOSE:

ACTION STEPS I CAN TAKE TODAY:

- ☐
- ☐
- ☐
- ☐
- ☐
- ☐

A SELF-CARE GOAL FOR TODAY:

A CHALLENGE I'M FACING:

SOMETHING I'M EXCITED ABOUT:

HOW I SPENT MY TIME TODAY:

- ☐ MY LIFE'S PASSION
- ☐ VOLUNTEERING
- ☐ ONLINE/SOCIAL MEDIA
- ☐ WORKING
- ☐ SELF-CARE
- ☐ DOWN TIME
- ☐ TIME WITH FRIENDS/FAMILY
- ☐ TIME OUTDOORS
- ☐ OTHER: _____

EVENING REFLECTION

HOW I'M FEELING:

THIS BROUGHT ME THE GREATEST JOY TODAY:

SOMETHING I DID TODAY THAT FELT MEANINGFUL:

WHAT I DID TODAY THAT ALIGNED WITH MY PURPOSE:

A NOTABLE RESULT FROM LIVING MY PURPOSE:

A SETBACK I FACED TODAY AND HOW I CAN LEARN OR GROW FROM THIS:

MORNING REFLECTION

DATE ___/___/___

MY PURPOSE OR INTENTION FOR TODAY:

GOALS ALIGNED WITH MY PURPOSE:

ACTION STEPS I CAN TAKE TODAY:

- ☐
- ☐
- ☐
- ☐
- ☐
- ☐

A SELF-CARE GOAL FOR TODAY:

A CHALLENGE I'M FACING:

SOMETHING I'M EXCITED ABOUT:

HOW I SPENT MY TIME TODAY:

- ☐ MY LIFE'S PASSION
- ☐ VOLUNTEERING
- ☐ ONLINE/SOCIAL MEDIA
- ☐ WORKING
- ☐ SELF-CARE
- ☐ DOWN TIME
- ☐ TIME WITH FRIENDS/FAMILY
- ☐ TIME OUTDOORS
- ☐ OTHER: _____

EVENING REFLECTION

HOW I'M FEELING:

THIS BROUGHT ME THE GREATEST JOY TODAY:

SOMETHING I DID TODAY THAT FELT MEANINGFUL:

WHAT I DID TODAY THAT ALIGNED WITH MY PURPOSE:

A NOTABLE RESULT FROM LIVING MY PURPOSE:

A SETBACK I FACED TODAY AND HOW I CAN LEARN OR GROW FROM THIS:

MORNING REFLECTION

DATE ___/___/___

MY PURPOSE OR INTENTION FOR TODAY:

GOALS ALIGNED WITH MY PURPOSE:

ACTION STEPS I CAN TAKE TODAY:

- ☐
- ☐
- ☐
- ☐
- ☐
- ☐

A SELF-CARE GOAL FOR TODAY:

A CHALLENGE I'M FACING:

SOMETHING I'M EXCITED ABOUT:

HOW I SPENT MY TIME TODAY:

- ☐ MY LIFE'S PASSION
- ☐ VOLUNTEERING
- ☐ ONLINE/SOCIAL MEDIA
- ☐ WORKING
- ☐ SELF-CARE
- ☐ DOWN TIME
- ☐ TIME WITH FRIENDS/FAMILY
- ☐ TIME OUTDOORS
- ☐ OTHER: _____

EVENING REFLECTION

HOW I'M FEELING:

THIS BROUGHT ME THE GREATEST JOY TODAY:

SOMETHING I DID TODAY THAT FELT MEANINGFUL:

WHAT I DID TODAY THAT ALIGNED WITH MY PURPOSE:

A NOTABLE RESULT FROM LIVING MY PURPOSE:

A SETBACK I FACED TODAY AND HOW I CAN LEARN OR GROW FROM THIS:

MORNING REFLECTION

DATE ___/___/___

MY PURPOSE OR INTENTION FOR TODAY:

GOALS ALIGNED WITH MY PURPOSE:

ACTION STEPS I CAN TAKE TODAY:

- ☐
- ☐
- ☐
- ☐
- ☐
- ☐

A SELF-CARE GOAL FOR TODAY:

A CHALLENGE I'M FACING:

SOMETHING I'M EXCITED ABOUT:

HOW I SPENT MY TIME TODAY:

- ☐ MY LIFE'S PASSION
- ☐ VOLUNTEERING
- ☐ ONLINE/SOCIAL MEDIA
- ☐ WORKING
- ☐ SELF-CARE
- ☐ DOWN TIME
- ☐ TIME WITH FRIENDS/FAMILY
- ☐ TIME OUTDOORS
- ☐ OTHER: _____

EVENING REFLECTION

HOW I'M FEELING:

THIS BROUGHT ME THE GREATEST JOY TODAY:

SOMETHING I DID TODAY THAT FELT MEANINGFUL:

WHAT I DID TODAY THAT ALIGNED WITH MY PURPOSE:

A NOTABLE RESULT FROM LIVING MY PURPOSE:

A SETBACK I FACED TODAY AND HOW I CAN LEARN OR GROW FROM THIS:

MORNING REFLECTION

DATE ___/___/___

MY PURPOSE OR INTENTION FOR TODAY:

GOALS ALIGNED WITH MY PURPOSE:

ACTION STEPS I CAN TAKE TODAY:

- ☐
- ☐
- ☐
- ☐
- ☐
- ☐

A SELF-CARE GOAL FOR TODAY:

A CHALLENGE I'M FACING:

SOMETHING I'M EXCITED ABOUT:

HOW I SPENT MY TIME TODAY:

- ☐ MY LIFE'S PASSION
- ☐ VOLUNTEERING
- ☐ ONLINE/SOCIAL MEDIA
- ☐ WORKING
- ☐ SELF-CARE
- ☐ DOWN TIME
- ☐ TIME WITH FRIENDS/FAMILY
- ☐ TIME OUTDOORS
- ☐ OTHER: _____

EVENING REFLECTION

HOW I'M FEELING:

THIS BROUGHT ME THE GREATEST JOY TODAY:

SOMETHING I DID TODAY THAT FELT MEANINGFUL:

WHAT I DID TODAY THAT ALIGNED WITH MY PURPOSE:

A NOTABLE RESULT FROM LIVING MY PURPOSE:

A SETBACK I FACED TODAY AND HOW I CAN LEARN OR GROW FROM THIS:

MORNING REFLECTION

DATE ___/___/___

MY PURPOSE OR INTENTION FOR TODAY:

GOALS ALIGNED WITH MY PURPOSE:

ACTION STEPS I CAN TAKE TODAY:

- ☐
- ☐
- ☐
- ☐
- ☐
- ☐

A SELF-CARE GOAL FOR TODAY:

A CHALLENGE I'M FACING:

SOMETHING I'M EXCITED ABOUT:

HOW I SPENT MY TIME TODAY:

- ☐ MY LIFE'S PASSION
- ☐ VOLUNTEERING
- ☐ ONLINE/SOCIAL MEDIA
- ☐ WORKING
- ☐ SELF-CARE
- ☐ DOWN TIME
- ☐ TIME WITH FRIENDS/FAMILY
- ☐ TIME OUTDOORS
- ☐ OTHER: _____

EVENING REFLECTION

HOW I'M FEELING:

THIS BROUGHT ME THE GREATEST JOY TODAY:

SOMETHING I DID TODAY THAT FELT MEANINGFUL:

WHAT I DID TODAY THAT ALIGNED WITH MY PURPOSE:

A NOTABLE RESULT FROM LIVING MY PURPOSE:

A SETBACK I FACED TODAY AND HOW I CAN LEARN OR GROW FROM THIS:

MORNING REFLECTION

DATE ___/___/___

MY PURPOSE OR INTENTION FOR TODAY:

GOALS ALIGNED WITH MY PURPOSE:

ACTION STEPS I CAN TAKE TODAY:

- ☐
- ☐
- ☐
- ☐
- ☐
- ☐

A SELF-CARE GOAL FOR TODAY:

A CHALLENGE I'M FACING:

SOMETHING I'M EXCITED ABOUT:

HOW I SPENT MY TIME TODAY:

- ☐ MY LIFE'S PASSION
- ☐ VOLUNTEERING
- ☐ ONLINE/SOCIAL MEDIA
- ☐ WORKING
- ☐ SELF-CARE
- ☐ DOWN TIME
- ☐ TIME WITH FRIENDS/FAMILY
- ☐ TIME OUTDOORS
- ☐ OTHER: _____

EVENING REFLECTION

HOW I'M FEELING:

THIS BROUGHT ME THE GREATEST JOY TODAY:

SOMETHING I DID TODAY THAT FELT MEANINGFUL:

WHAT I DID TODAY THAT ALIGNED WITH MY PURPOSE:

A NOTABLE RESULT FROM LIVING MY PURPOSE:

A SETBACK I FACED TODAY AND HOW I CAN LEARN OR GROW FROM THIS:

MORNING REFLECTION

DATE ___/___/___

MY PURPOSE OR INTENTION FOR TODAY:

GOALS ALIGNED WITH MY PURPOSE:

ACTION STEPS I CAN TAKE TODAY:

- ☐
- ☐
- ☐
- ☐
- ☐
- ☐

A SELF-CARE GOAL FOR TODAY:

A CHALLENGE I'M FACING:

SOMETHING I'M EXCITED ABOUT:

HOW I SPENT MY TIME TODAY:

- ☐ MY LIFE'S PASSION
- ☐ VOLUNTEERING
- ☐ ONLINE/SOCIAL MEDIA
- ☐ WORKING
- ☐ SELF-CARE
- ☐ DOWN TIME
- ☐ TIME WITH FRIENDS/FAMILY
- ☐ TIME OUTDOORS
- ☐ OTHER: _____

EVENING REFLECTION

HOW I'M FEELING:

THIS BROUGHT ME THE GREATEST JOY TODAY:

SOMETHING I DID TODAY THAT FELT MEANINGFUL:

WHAT I DID TODAY THAT ALIGNED WITH MY PURPOSE:

A NOTABLE RESULT FROM LIVING MY PURPOSE:

A SETBACK I FACED TODAY AND HOW I CAN LEARN OR GROW FROM THIS:

MORNING REFLECTION

DATE ___/___/___

MY PURPOSE OR INTENTION FOR TODAY:

GOALS ALIGNED WITH MY PURPOSE:

ACTION STEPS I CAN TAKE TODAY:

- ☐
- ☐
- ☐
- ☐
- ☐
- ☐

A SELF-CARE GOAL FOR TODAY:

A CHALLENGE I'M FACING:

SOMETHING I'M EXCITED ABOUT:

HOW I SPENT MY TIME TODAY:

- ☐ MY LIFE'S PASSION
- ☐ VOLUNTEERING
- ☐ ONLINE/SOCIAL MEDIA
- ☐ WORKING
- ☐ SELF-CARE
- ☐ DOWN TIME
- ☐ TIME WITH FRIENDS/FAMILY
- ☐ TIME OUTDOORS
- ☐ OTHER: _____

EVENING REFLECTION

HOW I'M FEELING:

THIS BROUGHT ME THE GREATEST JOY TODAY:

SOMETHING I DID TODAY THAT FELT MEANINGFUL:

WHAT I DID TODAY THAT ALIGNED WITH MY PURPOSE:

A NOTABLE RESULT FROM LIVING MY PURPOSE:

A SETBACK I FACED TODAY AND HOW I CAN LEARN OR GROW FROM THIS:

MORNING REFLECTION

DATE ___/___/___

MY PURPOSE OR INTENTION FOR TODAY:

GOALS ALIGNED WITH MY PURPOSE:

ACTION STEPS I CAN TAKE TODAY:

- ☐
- ☐
- ☐
- ☐
- ☐
- ☐

A SELF-CARE GOAL FOR TODAY:

A CHALLENGE I'M FACING:

SOMETHING I'M EXCITED ABOUT:

HOW I SPENT MY TIME TODAY:

- ☐ MY LIFE'S PASSION
- ☐ VOLUNTEERING
- ☐ ONLINE/SOCIAL MEDIA
- ☐ WORKING
- ☐ SELF-CARE
- ☐ DOWN TIME
- ☐ TIME WITH FRIENDS/FAMILY
- ☐ TIME OUTDOORS
- ☐ OTHER: _____

EVENING REFLECTION

HOW I'M FEELING:

THIS BROUGHT ME THE GREATEST JOY TODAY:

SOMETHING I DID TODAY THAT FELT MEANINGFUL:

WHAT I DID TODAY THAT ALIGNED WITH MY PURPOSE:

A NOTABLE RESULT FROM LIVING MY PURPOSE:

A SETBACK I FACED TODAY AND HOW I CAN LEARN OR GROW FROM THIS:

MORNING REFLECTION

DATE ___/___/___

MY PURPOSE OR INTENTION FOR TODAY:

GOALS ALIGNED WITH MY PURPOSE:

ACTION STEPS I CAN TAKE TODAY:

- ☐
- ☐
- ☐
- ☐
- ☐
- ☐

A SELF-CARE GOAL FOR TODAY:

A CHALLENGE I'M FACING:

SOMETHING I'M EXCITED ABOUT:

HOW I SPENT MY TIME TODAY:

- ☐ MY LIFE'S PASSION
- ☐ VOLUNTEERING
- ☐ ONLINE/SOCIAL MEDIA
- ☐ WORKING
- ☐ SELF-CARE
- ☐ DOWN TIME
- ☐ TIME WITH FRIENDS/FAMILY
- ☐ TIME OUTDOORS
- ☐ OTHER: _____

EVENING REFLECTION

HOW I'M FEELING:

THIS BROUGHT ME THE GREATEST JOY TODAY:

SOMETHING I DID TODAY THAT FELT MEANINGFUL:

WHAT I DID TODAY THAT ALIGNED WITH MY PURPOSE:

A NOTABLE RESULT FROM LIVING MY PURPOSE:

A SETBACK I FACED TODAY AND HOW I CAN LEARN OR GROW FROM THIS:

MORNING REFLECTION

DATE ___/___/___

MY PURPOSE OR INTENTION FOR TODAY:

GOALS ALIGNED WITH MY PURPOSE:

ACTION STEPS I CAN TAKE TODAY:

- ☐
- ☐
- ☐
- ☐
- ☐
- ☐

A SELF-CARE GOAL FOR TODAY:

A CHALLENGE I'M FACING:

SOMETHING I'M EXCITED ABOUT:

HOW I SPENT MY TIME TODAY:

- ☐ MY LIFE'S PASSION
- ☐ VOLUNTEERING
- ☐ ONLINE/SOCIAL MEDIA
- ☐ WORKING
- ☐ SELF-CARE
- ☐ DOWN TIME
- ☐ TIME WITH FRIENDS/FAMILY
- ☐ TIME OUTDOORS
- ☐ OTHER: _____

EVENING REFLECTION

HOW I'M FEELING:

THIS BROUGHT ME THE GREATEST JOY TODAY:

SOMETHING I DID TODAY THAT FELT MEANINGFUL:

WHAT I DID TODAY THAT ALIGNED WITH MY PURPOSE:

A NOTABLE RESULT FROM LIVING MY PURPOSE:

A SETBACK I FACED TODAY AND HOW I CAN LEARN OR GROW FROM THIS:

MORNING REFLECTION

DATE ___/___/___

MY PURPOSE OR INTENTION FOR TODAY:

GOALS ALIGNED WITH MY PURPOSE:

ACTION STEPS I CAN TAKE TODAY:

- ☐
- ☐
- ☐
- ☐
- ☐
- ☐

A SELF-CARE GOAL FOR TODAY:

A CHALLENGE I'M FACING:

SOMETHING I'M EXCITED ABOUT:

HOW I SPENT MY TIME TODAY:

- ☐ MY LIFE'S PASSION
- ☐ VOLUNTEERING
- ☐ ONLINE/SOCIAL MEDIA
- ☐ WORKING
- ☐ SELF-CARE
- ☐ DOWN TIME
- ☐ TIME WITH FRIENDS/FAMILY
- ☐ TIME OUTDOORS
- ☐ OTHER: _____

EVENING REFLECTION

HOW I'M FEELING:

THIS BROUGHT ME THE GREATEST JOY TODAY:

SOMETHING I DID TODAY THAT FELT MEANINGFUL:

WHAT I DID TODAY THAT ALIGNED WITH MY PURPOSE:

A NOTABLE RESULT FROM LIVING MY PURPOSE:

A SETBACK I FACED TODAY AND HOW I CAN LEARN OR GROW FROM THIS:

MORNING REFLECTION

DATE ___/___/___

MY PURPOSE OR INTENTION FOR TODAY:

GOALS ALIGNED WITH MY PURPOSE:

ACTION STEPS I CAN TAKE TODAY:

- ☐
- ☐
- ☐
- ☐
- ☐
- ☐

A SELF-CARE GOAL FOR TODAY:

A CHALLENGE I'M FACING:

SOMETHING I'M EXCITED ABOUT:

HOW I SPENT MY TIME TODAY:

- ☐ MY LIFE'S PASSION
- ☐ VOLUNTEERING
- ☐ ONLINE/SOCIAL MEDIA
- ☐ WORKING
- ☐ SELF-CARE
- ☐ DOWN TIME
- ☐ TIME WITH FRIENDS/FAMILY
- ☐ TIME OUTDOORS
- ☐ OTHER: _____

EVENING REFLECTION

HOW I'M FEELING:

THIS BROUGHT ME THE GREATEST JOY TODAY:

SOMETHING I DID TODAY THAT FELT MEANINGFUL:

WHAT I DID TODAY THAT ALIGNED WITH MY PURPOSE:

A NOTABLE RESULT FROM LIVING MY PURPOSE:

A SETBACK I FACED TODAY AND HOW I CAN LEARN OR GROW FROM THIS:

MORNING REFLECTION

DATE ___/___/___

MY PURPOSE OR INTENTION FOR TODAY:

GOALS ALIGNED WITH MY PURPOSE:

ACTION STEPS I CAN TAKE TODAY:

- ☐
- ☐
- ☐
- ☐
- ☐
- ☐

A SELF-CARE GOAL FOR TODAY:

A CHALLENGE I'M FACING:

SOMETHING I'M EXCITED ABOUT:

HOW I SPENT MY TIME TODAY:

- ☐ MY LIFE'S PASSION
- ☐ VOLUNTEERING
- ☐ ONLINE/SOCIAL MEDIA
- ☐ WORKING
- ☐ SELF-CARE
- ☐ DOWN TIME
- ☐ TIME WITH FRIENDS/FAMILY
- ☐ TIME OUTDOORS
- ☐ OTHER: _____

EVENING REFLECTION

HOW I'M FEELING:

THIS BROUGHT ME THE GREATEST JOY TODAY:

SOMETHING I DID TODAY THAT FELT MEANINGFUL:

WHAT I DID TODAY THAT ALIGNED WITH MY PURPOSE:

A NOTABLE RESULT FROM LIVING MY PURPOSE:

A SETBACK I FACED TODAY AND HOW I CAN LEARN OR GROW FROM THIS:

MORNING REFLECTION

DATE ___/___/___

MY PURPOSE OR INTENTION FOR TODAY:

GOALS ALIGNED WITH MY PURPOSE:

ACTION STEPS I CAN TAKE TODAY:

- ☐
- ☐
- ☐
- ☐
- ☐
- ☐

A SELF-CARE GOAL FOR TODAY:

A CHALLENGE I'M FACING:

SOMETHING I'M EXCITED ABOUT:

HOW I SPENT MY TIME TODAY:

- ☐ MY LIFE'S PASSION
- ☐ VOLUNTEERING
- ☐ ONLINE/SOCIAL MEDIA
- ☐ WORKING
- ☐ SELF-CARE
- ☐ DOWN TIME
- ☐ TIME WITH FRIENDS/FAMILY
- ☐ TIME OUTDOORS
- ☐ OTHER: _____

EVENING REFLECTION

HOW I'M FEELING:

THIS BROUGHT ME THE GREATEST JOY TODAY:

SOMETHING I DID TODAY THAT FELT MEANINGFUL:

WHAT I DID TODAY THAT ALIGNED WITH MY PURPOSE:

A NOTABLE RESULT FROM LIVING MY PURPOSE:

A SETBACK I FACED TODAY AND HOW I CAN LEARN OR GROW FROM THIS:

MORNING REFLECTION

DATE ___/___/___

MY PURPOSE OR INTENTION FOR TODAY:

GOALS ALIGNED WITH MY PURPOSE:

ACTION STEPS I CAN TAKE TODAY:

- ☐
- ☐
- ☐
- ☐
- ☐
- ☐

A SELF-CARE GOAL FOR TODAY:

A CHALLENGE I'M FACING:

SOMETHING I'M EXCITED ABOUT:

HOW I SPENT MY TIME TODAY:

- ☐ MY LIFE'S PASSION
- ☐ VOLUNTEERING
- ☐ ONLINE/SOCIAL MEDIA
- ☐ WORKING
- ☐ SELF-CARE
- ☐ DOWN TIME
- ☐ TIME WITH FRIENDS/FAMILY
- ☐ TIME OUTDOORS
- ☐ OTHER: _____

EVENING REFLECTION

HOW I'M FEELING:

THIS BROUGHT ME THE GREATEST JOY TODAY:

SOMETHING I DID TODAY THAT FELT MEANINGFUL:

WHAT I DID TODAY THAT ALIGNED WITH MY PURPOSE:

A NOTABLE RESULT FROM LIVING MY PURPOSE:

A SETBACK I FACED TODAY AND HOW I CAN LEARN OR GROW FROM THIS:

MORNING REFLECTION

DATE ___/___/___

MY PURPOSE OR INTENTION FOR TODAY:

GOALS ALIGNED WITH MY PURPOSE:

ACTION STEPS I CAN TAKE TODAY:

- ☐
- ☐
- ☐
- ☐
- ☐
- ☐

A SELF-CARE GOAL FOR TODAY:

A CHALLENGE I'M FACING:

SOMETHING I'M EXCITED ABOUT:

HOW I SPENT MY TIME TODAY:

- ☐ MY LIFE'S PASSION
- ☐ WORKING
- ☐ TIME WITH FRIENDS/FAMILY
- ☐ VOLUNTEERING
- ☐ SELF-CARE
- ☐ TIME OUTDOORS
- ☐ ONLINE/SOCIAL MEDIA
- ☐ DOWN TIME
- ☐ OTHER: _____

EVENING REFLECTION

HOW I'M FEELING:

THIS BROUGHT ME THE GREATEST JOY TODAY:

SOMETHING I DID TODAY THAT FELT MEANINGFUL:

WHAT I DID TODAY THAT ALIGNED WITH MY PURPOSE:

A NOTABLE RESULT FROM LIVING MY PURPOSE:

A SETBACK I FACED TODAY AND HOW I CAN LEARN OR GROW FROM THIS:

MORNING REFLECTION

DATE ___/___/___

MY PURPOSE OR INTENTION FOR TODAY:

GOALS ALIGNED WITH MY PURPOSE:

ACTION STEPS I CAN TAKE TODAY:

- ☐
- ☐
- ☐
- ☐
- ☐
- ☐

A SELF-CARE GOAL FOR TODAY:

A CHALLENGE I'M FACING:

SOMETHING I'M EXCITED ABOUT:

HOW I SPENT MY TIME TODAY:

- ☐ MY LIFE'S PASSION
- ☐ VOLUNTEERING
- ☐ ONLINE/SOCIAL MEDIA
- ☐ WORKING
- ☐ SELF-CARE
- ☐ DOWN TIME
- ☐ TIME WITH FRIENDS/FAMILY
- ☐ TIME OUTDOORS
- ☐ OTHER: _____

EVENING REFLECTION

HOW I'M FEELING:

THIS BROUGHT ME THE GREATEST JOY TODAY:

SOMETHING I DID TODAY THAT FELT MEANINGFUL:

WHAT I DID TODAY THAT ALIGNED WITH MY PURPOSE:

A NOTABLE RESULT FROM LIVING MY PURPOSE:

A SETBACK I FACED TODAY AND HOW I CAN LEARN OR GROW FROM THIS:

MORNING REFLECTION

DATE ___/___/___

MY PURPOSE OR INTENTION FOR TODAY:

GOALS ALIGNED WITH MY PURPOSE:

ACTION STEPS I CAN TAKE TODAY:

- ☐
- ☐
- ☐
- ☐
- ☐
- ☐

A SELF-CARE GOAL FOR TODAY:

A CHALLENGE I'M FACING:

SOMETHING I'M EXCITED ABOUT:

HOW I SPENT MY TIME TODAY:

- ☐ MY LIFE'S PASSION
- ☐ VOLUNTEERING
- ☐ ONLINE/SOCIAL MEDIA
- ☐ WORKING
- ☐ SELF-CARE
- ☐ DOWN TIME
- ☐ TIME WITH FRIENDS/FAMILY
- ☐ TIME OUTDOORS
- ☐ OTHER: _____

EVENING REFLECTION

HOW I'M FEELING:

THIS BROUGHT ME THE GREATEST JOY TODAY:

SOMETHING I DID TODAY THAT FELT MEANINGFUL:

WHAT I DID TODAY THAT ALIGNED WITH MY PURPOSE:

A NOTABLE RESULT FROM LIVING MY PURPOSE:

A SETBACK I FACED TODAY AND HOW I CAN LEARN OR GROW FROM THIS:

MORNING REFLECTION

DATE ___/___/___

MY PURPOSE OR INTENTION FOR TODAY:

GOALS ALIGNED WITH MY PURPOSE:

ACTION STEPS I CAN TAKE TODAY:

- ☐
- ☐
- ☐
- ☐
- ☐
- ☐

A SELF-CARE GOAL FOR TODAY:

A CHALLENGE I'M FACING:

SOMETHING I'M EXCITED ABOUT:

HOW I SPENT MY TIME TODAY:

- ☐ MY LIFE'S PASSION
- ☐ VOLUNTEERING
- ☐ ONLINE/SOCIAL MEDIA
- ☐ WORKING
- ☐ SELF-CARE
- ☐ DOWN TIME
- ☐ TIME WITH FRIENDS/FAMILY
- ☐ TIME OUTDOORS
- ☐ OTHER: _____

EVENING REFLECTION

HOW I'M FEELING:

THIS BROUGHT ME THE GREATEST JOY TODAY:

SOMETHING I DID TODAY THAT FELT MEANINGFUL:

WHAT I DID TODAY THAT ALIGNED WITH MY PURPOSE:

A NOTABLE RESULT FROM LIVING MY PURPOSE:

A SETBACK I FACED TODAY AND HOW I CAN LEARN OR GROW FROM THIS:

MORNING REFLECTION

DATE ___/___/___

MY PURPOSE OR INTENTION FOR TODAY:

GOALS ALIGNED WITH MY PURPOSE:

ACTION STEPS I CAN TAKE TODAY:

- ☐
- ☐
- ☐
- ☐
- ☐
- ☐

A SELF-CARE GOAL FOR TODAY:

A CHALLENGE I'M FACING:

SOMETHING I'M EXCITED ABOUT:

HOW I SPENT MY TIME TODAY:

- ☐ MY LIFE'S PASSION
- ☐ VOLUNTEERING
- ☐ ONLINE/SOCIAL MEDIA
- ☐ WORKING
- ☐ SELF-CARE
- ☐ DOWN TIME
- ☐ TIME WITH FRIENDS/FAMILY
- ☐ TIME OUTDOORS
- ☐ OTHER: _____

EVENING REFLECTION

HOW I'M FEELING:

THIS BROUGHT ME THE GREATEST JOY TODAY:

SOMETHING I DID TODAY THAT FELT MEANINGFUL:

WHAT I DID TODAY THAT ALIGNED WITH MY PURPOSE:

A NOTABLE RESULT FROM LIVING MY PURPOSE:

A SETBACK I FACED TODAY AND HOW I CAN LEARN OR GROW FROM THIS:

MORNING REFLECTION

DATE ___/___/___

MY PURPOSE OR INTENTION FOR TODAY:

GOALS ALIGNED WITH MY PURPOSE:

ACTION STEPS I CAN TAKE TODAY:

- ☐
- ☐
- ☐
- ☐
- ☐
- ☐

A SELF-CARE GOAL FOR TODAY:

A CHALLENGE I'M FACING:

SOMETHING I'M EXCITED ABOUT:

HOW I SPENT MY TIME TODAY:

- ☐ MY LIFE'S PASSION
- ☐ VOLUNTEERING
- ☐ ONLINE/SOCIAL MEDIA
- ☐ WORKING
- ☐ SELF-CARE
- ☐ DOWN TIME
- ☐ TIME WITH FRIENDS/FAMILY
- ☐ TIME OUTDOORS
- ☐ OTHER: _____

EVENING REFLECTION

HOW I'M FEELING:

THIS BROUGHT ME THE GREATEST JOY TODAY:

SOMETHING I DID TODAY THAT FELT MEANINGFUL:

WHAT I DID TODAY THAT ALIGNED WITH MY PURPOSE:

A NOTABLE RESULT FROM LIVING MY PURPOSE:

A SETBACK I FACED TODAY AND HOW I CAN LEARN OR GROW FROM THIS:

MORNING REFLECTION

DATE ___/___/___

MY PURPOSE OR INTENTION FOR TODAY:

GOALS ALIGNED WITH MY PURPOSE:

ACTION STEPS I CAN TAKE TODAY:

- ☐
- ☐
- ☐
- ☐
- ☐
- ☐

A SELF-CARE GOAL FOR TODAY:

A CHALLENGE I'M FACING:

SOMETHING I'M EXCITED ABOUT:

HOW I SPENT MY TIME TODAY:

- ☐ MY LIFE'S PASSION
- ☐ VOLUNTEERING
- ☐ ONLINE/SOCIAL MEDIA
- ☐ WORKING
- ☐ SELF-CARE
- ☐ DOWN TIME
- ☐ TIME WITH FRIENDS/FAMILY
- ☐ TIME OUTDOORS
- ☐ OTHER: _____

EVENING REFLECTION

HOW I'M FEELING:

THIS BROUGHT ME THE GREATEST JOY TODAY:

SOMETHING I DID TODAY THAT FELT MEANINGFUL:

WHAT I DID TODAY THAT ALIGNED WITH MY PURPOSE:

A NOTABLE RESULT FROM LIVING MY PURPOSE:

A SETBACK I FACED TODAY AND HOW I CAN LEARN OR GROW FROM THIS:

MORNING REFLECTION

DATE ___/___/___

MY PURPOSE OR INTENTION FOR TODAY:

GOALS ALIGNED WITH MY PURPOSE:

ACTION STEPS I CAN TAKE TODAY:

- ☐
- ☐
- ☐
- ☐
- ☐
- ☐

A SELF-CARE GOAL FOR TODAY:

A CHALLENGE I'M FACING:

SOMETHING I'M EXCITED ABOUT:

HOW I SPENT MY TIME TODAY:

- ☐ MY LIFE'S PASSION
- ☐ VOLUNTEERING
- ☐ ONLINE/SOCIAL MEDIA
- ☐ WORKING
- ☐ SELF-CARE
- ☐ DOWN TIME
- ☐ TIME WITH FRIENDS/FAMILY
- ☐ TIME OUTDOORS
- ☐ OTHER: _____

EVENING REFLECTION

HOW I'M FEELING:

THIS BROUGHT ME THE GREATEST JOY TODAY:

SOMETHING I DID TODAY THAT FELT MEANINGFUL:

WHAT I DID TODAY THAT ALIGNED WITH MY PURPOSE:

A NOTABLE RESULT FROM LIVING MY PURPOSE:

A SETBACK I FACED TODAY AND HOW I CAN LEARN OR GROW FROM THIS:

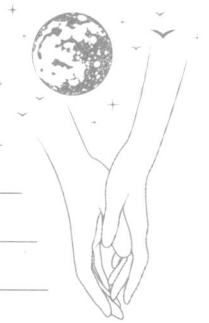

MORNING REFLECTION

DATE ___/___/___

MY PURPOSE OR INTENTION FOR TODAY:

GOALS ALIGNED WITH MY PURPOSE:

ACTION STEPS I CAN TAKE TODAY:

- ☐
- ☐
- ☐
- ☐
- ☐
- ☐

A SELF-CARE GOAL FOR TODAY:

A CHALLENGE I'M FACING:

SOMETHING I'M EXCITED ABOUT:

HOW I SPENT MY TIME TODAY:

- ☐ MY LIFE'S PASSION
- ☐ VOLUNTEERING
- ☐ ONLINE/SOCIAL MEDIA
- ☐ WORKING
- ☐ SELF-CARE
- ☐ DOWN TIME
- ☐ TIME WITH FRIENDS/FAMILY
- ☐ TIME OUTDOORS
- ☐ OTHER: _____

EVENING REFLECTION

HOW I'M FEELING:

THIS BROUGHT ME THE GREATEST JOY TODAY:

SOMETHING I DID TODAY THAT FELT MEANINGFUL:

WHAT I DID TODAY THAT ALIGNED WITH MY PURPOSE:

A NOTABLE RESULT FROM LIVING MY PURPOSE:

A SETBACK I FACED TODAY AND HOW I CAN LEARN OR GROW FROM THIS:

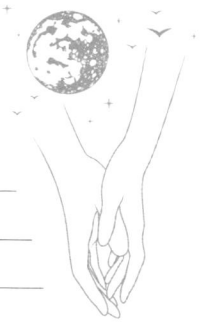

MORNING REFLECTION

DATE ___/___/___

MY PURPOSE OR INTENTION FOR TODAY:

GOALS ALIGNED WITH MY PURPOSE:

ACTION STEPS I CAN TAKE TODAY:

- ☐
- ☐
- ☐
- ☐
- ☐
- ☐

A SELF-CARE GOAL FOR TODAY:

A CHALLENGE I'M FACING:

SOMETHING I'M EXCITED ABOUT:

HOW I SPENT MY TIME TODAY:

- ☐ MY LIFE'S PASSION
- ☐ VOLUNTEERING
- ☐ ONLINE/SOCIAL MEDIA
- ☐ WORKING
- ☐ SELF-CARE
- ☐ DOWN TIME
- ☐ TIME WITH FRIENDS/FAMILY
- ☐ TIME OUTDOORS
- ☐ OTHER: _____

EVENING REFLECTION

HOW I'M FEELING:

THIS BROUGHT ME THE GREATEST JOY TODAY:

SOMETHING I DID TODAY THAT FELT MEANINGFUL:

WHAT I DID TODAY THAT ALIGNED WITH MY PURPOSE:

A NOTABLE RESULT FROM LIVING MY PURPOSE:

A SETBACK I FACED TODAY AND HOW I CAN LEARN OR GROW FROM THIS:

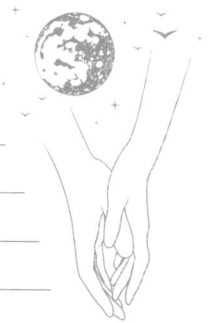

MORNING REFLECTION

DATE ___/___/___

MY PURPOSE OR INTENTION FOR TODAY:

GOALS ALIGNED WITH MY PURPOSE:

ACTION STEPS I CAN TAKE TODAY:

- ☐
- ☐
- ☐
- ☐
- ☐
- ☐

A SELF-CARE GOAL FOR TODAY:

A CHALLENGE I'M FACING:

SOMETHING I'M EXCITED ABOUT:

HOW I SPENT MY TIME TODAY:

- ☐ MY LIFE'S PASSION
- ☐ VOLUNTEERING
- ☐ ONLINE/SOCIAL MEDIA
- ☐ WORKING
- ☐ SELF-CARE
- ☐ DOWN TIME
- ☐ TIME WITH FRIENDS/FAMILY
- ☐ TIME OUTDOORS
- ☐ OTHER: _____

EVENING REFLECTION

HOW I'M FEELING:

THIS BROUGHT ME THE GREATEST JOY TODAY:

SOMETHING I DID TODAY THAT FELT MEANINGFUL:

WHAT I DID TODAY THAT ALIGNED WITH MY PURPOSE:

A NOTABLE RESULT FROM LIVING MY PURPOSE:

A SETBACK I FACED TODAY AND HOW I CAN LEARN OR GROW FROM THIS:

MORNING REFLECTION

DATE ___/___/___

MY PURPOSE OR INTENTION FOR TODAY:

GOALS ALIGNED WITH MY PURPOSE:

ACTION STEPS I CAN TAKE TODAY:

- ☐
- ☐
- ☐
- ☐
- ☐
- ☐

A SELF-CARE GOAL FOR TODAY:

A CHALLENGE I'M FACING:

SOMETHING I'M EXCITED ABOUT:

HOW I SPENT MY TIME TODAY:

- ☐ MY LIFE'S PASSION
- ☐ VOLUNTEERING
- ☐ ONLINE/SOCIAL MEDIA
- ☐ WORKING
- ☐ SELF-CARE
- ☐ DOWN TIME
- ☐ TIME WITH FRIENDS/FAMILY
- ☐ TIME OUTDOORS
- ☐ OTHER: _____

EVENING REFLECTION

HOW I'M FEELING:

THIS BROUGHT ME THE GREATEST JOY TODAY:

SOMETHING I DID TODAY THAT FELT MEANINGFUL:

WHAT I DID TODAY THAT ALIGNED WITH MY PURPOSE:

A NOTABLE RESULT FROM LIVING MY PURPOSE:

A SETBACK I FACED TODAY AND HOW I CAN LEARN OR GROW FROM THIS:

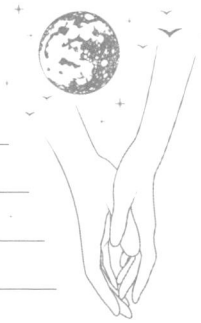

MORNING REFLECTION

DATE ___/___/___

MY PURPOSE OR INTENTION FOR TODAY:

GOALS ALIGNED WITH MY PURPOSE:

ACTION STEPS I CAN TAKE TODAY:

- ☐
- ☐
- ☐
- ☐
- ☐
- ☐

A SELF-CARE GOAL FOR TODAY:

A CHALLENGE I'M FACING:

SOMETHING I'M EXCITED ABOUT:

HOW I SPENT MY TIME TODAY:

- ☐ MY LIFE'S PASSION
- ☐ VOLUNTEERING
- ☐ ONLINE/SOCIAL MEDIA
- ☐ WORKING
- ☐ SELF-CARE
- ☐ DOWN TIME
- ☐ TIME WITH FRIENDS/FAMILY
- ☐ TIME OUTDOORS
- ☐ OTHER: _____

EVENING REFLECTION

HOW I'M FEELING:

THIS BROUGHT ME THE GREATEST JOY TODAY:

SOMETHING I DID TODAY THAT FELT MEANINGFUL:

WHAT I DID TODAY THAT ALIGNED WITH MY PURPOSE:

A NOTABLE RESULT FROM LIVING MY PURPOSE:

A SETBACK I FACED TODAY AND HOW I CAN LEARN OR GROW FROM THIS:

MORNING REFLECTION

DATE ___/___/___

MY PURPOSE OR INTENTION FOR TODAY:

GOALS ALIGNED WITH MY PURPOSE:

ACTION STEPS I CAN TAKE TODAY:

- ☐
- ☐
- ☐
- ☐
- ☐
- ☐

A SELF-CARE GOAL FOR TODAY:

A CHALLENGE I'M FACING:

SOMETHING I'M EXCITED ABOUT:

HOW I SPENT MY TIME TODAY:

- ☐ MY LIFE'S PASSION
- ☐ VOLUNTEERING
- ☐ ONLINE/SOCIAL MEDIA
- ☐ WORKING
- ☐ SELF-CARE
- ☐ DOWN TIME
- ☐ TIME WITH FRIENDS/FAMILY
- ☐ TIME OUTDOORS
- ☐ OTHER: _____

EVENING REFLECTION

HOW I'M FEELING:

THIS BROUGHT ME THE GREATEST JOY TODAY:

SOMETHING I DID TODAY THAT FELT MEANINGFUL:

WHAT I DID TODAY THAT ALIGNED WITH MY PURPOSE:

A NOTABLE RESULT FROM LIVING MY PURPOSE:

A SETBACK I FACED TODAY AND HOW I CAN LEARN OR GROW FROM THIS:

MORNING REFLECTION

DATE ___/___/___

MY PURPOSE OR INTENTION FOR TODAY:

GOALS ALIGNED WITH MY PURPOSE:

ACTION STEPS I CAN TAKE TODAY:

- ☐
- ☐
- ☐
- ☐
- ☐
- ☐

A SELF-CARE GOAL FOR TODAY:

A CHALLENGE I'M FACING:

SOMETHING I'M EXCITED ABOUT:

HOW I SPENT MY TIME TODAY:

- ☐ MY LIFE'S PASSION
- ☐ VOLUNTEERING
- ☐ ONLINE/SOCIAL MEDIA
- ☐ WORKING
- ☐ SELF-CARE
- ☐ DOWN TIME
- ☐ TIME WITH FRIENDS/FAMILY
- ☐ TIME OUTDOORS
- ☐ OTHER: _____

EVENING REFLECTION

HOW I'M FEELING:

THIS BROUGHT ME THE GREATEST JOY TODAY:

SOMETHING I DID TODAY THAT FELT MEANINGFUL:

WHAT I DID TODAY THAT ALIGNED WITH MY PURPOSE:

A NOTABLE RESULT FROM LIVING MY PURPOSE:

A SETBACK I FACED TODAY AND HOW I CAN LEARN OR GROW FROM THIS:

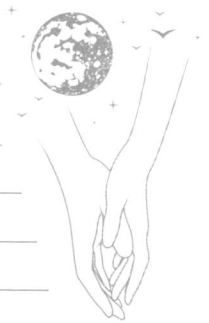

MORNING REFLECTION

DATE ___/___/___

MY PURPOSE OR INTENTION FOR TODAY:

GOALS ALIGNED WITH MY PURPOSE:

ACTION STEPS I CAN TAKE TODAY:

- ☐
- ☐
- ☐
- ☐
- ☐
- ☐

A SELF-CARE GOAL FOR TODAY:

A CHALLENGE I'M FACING:

SOMETHING I'M EXCITED ABOUT:

HOW I SPENT MY TIME TODAY:

- ☐ MY LIFE'S PASSION
- ☐ VOLUNTEERING
- ☐ ONLINE/SOCIAL MEDIA
- ☐ WORKING
- ☐ SELF-CARE
- ☐ DOWN TIME
- ☐ TIME WITH FRIENDS/FAMILY
- ☐ TIME OUTDOORS
- ☐ OTHER: _____

EVENING REFLECTION

HOW I'M FEELING:

THIS BROUGHT ME THE GREATEST JOY TODAY:

SOMETHING I DID TODAY THAT FELT MEANINGFUL:

WHAT I DID TODAY THAT ALIGNED WITH MY PURPOSE:

A NOTABLE RESULT FROM LIVING MY PURPOSE:

A SETBACK I FACED TODAY AND HOW I CAN LEARN OR GROW FROM THIS:

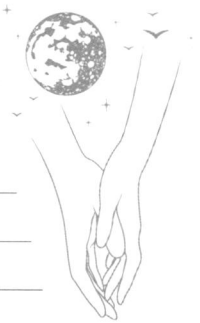

MORNING REFLECTION

DATE ___/___/___

MY PURPOSE OR INTENTION FOR TODAY:

GOALS ALIGNED WITH MY PURPOSE:

ACTION STEPS I CAN TAKE TODAY:

- ☐
- ☐
- ☐
- ☐
- ☐
- ☐

A SELF-CARE GOAL FOR TODAY:

A CHALLENGE I'M FACING:

SOMETHING I'M EXCITED ABOUT:

HOW I SPENT MY TIME TODAY:

- ☐ MY LIFE'S PASSION
- ☐ VOLUNTEERING
- ☐ ONLINE/SOCIAL MEDIA
- ☐ WORKING
- ☐ SELF-CARE
- ☐ DOWN TIME
- ☐ TIME WITH FRIENDS/FAMILY
- ☐ TIME OUTDOORS
- ☐ OTHER: _____

EVENING REFLECTION

HOW I'M FEELING:

THIS BROUGHT ME THE GREATEST JOY TODAY:

SOMETHING I DID TODAY THAT FELT MEANINGFUL:

WHAT I DID TODAY THAT ALIGNED WITH MY PURPOSE:

A NOTABLE RESULT FROM LIVING MY PURPOSE:

A SETBACK I FACED TODAY AND HOW I CAN LEARN OR GROW FROM THIS:

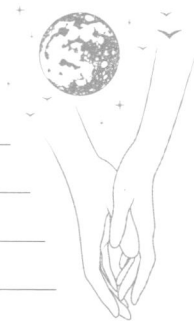

MORNING REFLECTION

DATE ___/___/___

MY PURPOSE OR INTENTION FOR TODAY:

GOALS ALIGNED WITH MY PURPOSE:

ACTION STEPS I CAN TAKE TODAY:

- ☐
- ☐
- ☐
- ☐
- ☐
- ☐

A SELF-CARE GOAL FOR TODAY:

A CHALLENGE I'M FACING:

SOMETHING I'M EXCITED ABOUT:

HOW I SPENT MY TIME TODAY:

- ☐ MY LIFE'S PASSION
- ☐ VOLUNTEERING
- ☐ ONLINE/SOCIAL MEDIA
- ☐ WORKING
- ☐ SELF-CARE
- ☐ DOWN TIME
- ☐ TIME WITH FRIENDS/FAMILY
- ☐ TIME OUTDOORS
- ☐ OTHER: _____

EVENING REFLECTION

HOW I'M FEELING:

THIS BROUGHT ME THE GREATEST JOY TODAY:

SOMETHING I DID TODAY THAT FELT MEANINGFUL:

WHAT I DID TODAY THAT ALIGNED WITH MY PURPOSE:

A NOTABLE RESULT FROM LIVING MY PURPOSE:

A SETBACK I FACED TODAY AND HOW I CAN LEARN OR GROW FROM THIS:

MORNING REFLECTION

DATE ___/___/___

MY PURPOSE OR INTENTION FOR TODAY:

GOALS ALIGNED WITH MY PURPOSE:

ACTION STEPS I CAN TAKE TODAY:

- ☐
- ☐
- ☐
- ☐
- ☐
- ☐

A SELF-CARE GOAL FOR TODAY:

A CHALLENGE I'M FACING:

SOMETHING I'M EXCITED ABOUT:

HOW I SPENT MY TIME TODAY:

- ☐ MY LIFE'S PASSION
- ☐ VOLUNTEERING
- ☐ ONLINE/SOCIAL MEDIA
- ☐ WORKING
- ☐ SELF-CARE
- ☐ DOWN TIME
- ☐ TIME WITH FRIENDS/FAMILY
- ☐ TIME OUTDOORS
- ☐ OTHER: _____

EVENING REFLECTION

HOW I'M FEELING:

THIS BROUGHT ME THE GREATEST JOY TODAY:

SOMETHING I DID TODAY THAT FELT MEANINGFUL:

WHAT I DID TODAY THAT ALIGNED WITH MY PURPOSE:

A NOTABLE RESULT FROM LIVING MY PURPOSE:

A SETBACK I FACED TODAY AND HOW I CAN LEARN OR GROW FROM THIS:

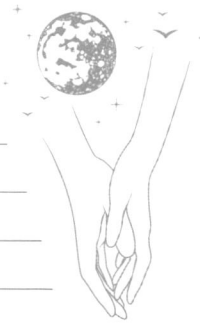

MORNING REFLECTION

DATE ___/___/___

MY PURPOSE OR INTENTION FOR TODAY:

GOALS ALIGNED WITH MY PURPOSE:

ACTION STEPS I CAN TAKE TODAY:

- ☐
- ☐
- ☐
- ☐
- ☐
- ☐

A SELF-CARE GOAL FOR TODAY:

A CHALLENGE I'M FACING:

SOMETHING I'M EXCITED ABOUT:

HOW I SPENT MY TIME TODAY:

- ☐ MY LIFE'S PASSION
- ☐ VOLUNTEERING
- ☐ ONLINE/SOCIAL MEDIA
- ☐ WORKING
- ☐ SELF-CARE
- ☐ DOWN TIME
- ☐ TIME WITH FRIENDS/FAMILY
- ☐ TIME OUTDOORS
- ☐ OTHER: _____

EVENING REFLECTION

HOW I'M FEELING:

THIS BROUGHT ME THE GREATEST JOY TODAY:

SOMETHING I DID TODAY THAT FELT MEANINGFUL:

WHAT I DID TODAY THAT ALIGNED WITH MY PURPOSE:

A NOTABLE RESULT FROM LIVING MY PURPOSE:

A SETBACK I FACED TODAY AND HOW I CAN LEARN OR GROW FROM THIS:

MORNING REFLECTION

DATE ___/___/___

MY PURPOSE OR INTENTION FOR TODAY:

GOALS ALIGNED WITH MY PURPOSE:

ACTION STEPS I CAN TAKE TODAY:

- ☐
- ☐
- ☐
- ☐
- ☐
- ☐

A SELF-CARE GOAL FOR TODAY:

A CHALLENGE I'M FACING:

SOMETHING I'M EXCITED ABOUT:

HOW I SPENT MY TIME TODAY:

- ☐ MY LIFE'S PASSION
- ☐ VOLUNTEERING
- ☐ ONLINE/SOCIAL MEDIA
- ☐ WORKING
- ☐ SELF-CARE
- ☐ DOWN TIME
- ☐ TIME WITH FRIENDS/FAMILY
- ☐ TIME OUTDOORS
- ☐ OTHER: _____

EVENING REFLECTION

HOW I'M FEELING:

THIS BROUGHT ME THE GREATEST JOY TODAY:

SOMETHING I DID TODAY THAT FELT MEANINGFUL:

WHAT I DID TODAY THAT ALIGNED WITH MY PURPOSE:

A NOTABLE RESULT FROM LIVING MY PURPOSE:

A SETBACK I FACED TODAY AND HOW I CAN LEARN OR GROW FROM THIS:

MORNING REFLECTION

DATE ___/___/___

MY PURPOSE OR INTENTION FOR TODAY:

GOALS ALIGNED WITH MY PURPOSE:

ACTION STEPS I CAN TAKE TODAY:

- ☐
- ☐
- ☐
- ☐
- ☐
- ☐

A SELF-CARE GOAL FOR TODAY:

A CHALLENGE I'M FACING:

SOMETHING I'M EXCITED ABOUT:

HOW I SPENT MY TIME TODAY:

- ☐ MY LIFE'S PASSION
- ☐ VOLUNTEERING
- ☐ ONLINE/SOCIAL MEDIA
- ☐ WORKING
- ☐ SELF-CARE
- ☐ DOWN TIME
- ☐ TIME WITH FRIENDS/FAMILY
- ☐ TIME OUTDOORS
- ☐ OTHER: _____

EVENING REFLECTION

HOW I'M FEELING:

THIS BROUGHT ME THE GREATEST JOY TODAY:

SOMETHING I DID TODAY THAT FELT MEANINGFUL:

WHAT I DID TODAY THAT ALIGNED WITH MY PURPOSE:

A NOTABLE RESULT FROM LIVING MY PURPOSE:

A SETBACK I FACED TODAY AND HOW I CAN LEARN OR GROW FROM THIS:

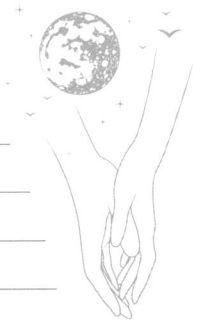

MORNING REFLECTION

DATE ___/___/___

MY PURPOSE OR INTENTION FOR TODAY:

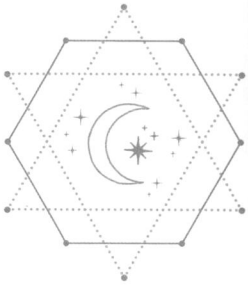

GOALS ALIGNED WITH MY PURPOSE:

ACTION STEPS I CAN TAKE TODAY:

- ☐
- ☐
- ☐
- ☐
- ☐
- ☐

A SELF-CARE GOAL FOR TODAY:

A CHALLENGE I'M FACING:

SOMETHING I'M EXCITED ABOUT:

HOW I SPENT MY TIME TODAY:

- ☐ MY LIFE'S PASSION
- ☐ VOLUNTEERING
- ☐ ONLINE/SOCIAL MEDIA
- ☐ WORKING
- ☐ SELF-CARE
- ☐ DOWN TIME
- ☐ TIME WITH FRIENDS/FAMILY
- ☐ TIME OUTDOORS
- ☐ OTHER: _____

EVENING REFLECTION

HOW I'M FEELING:

THIS BROUGHT ME THE GREATEST JOY TODAY:

SOMETHING I DID TODAY THAT FELT MEANINGFUL:

WHAT I DID TODAY THAT ALIGNED WITH MY PURPOSE:

A NOTABLE RESULT FROM LIVING MY PURPOSE:

A SETBACK I FACED TODAY AND HOW I CAN LEARN OR GROW FROM THIS:

MORNING REFLECTION

DATE ___/___/___

MY PURPOSE OR INTENTION FOR TODAY:

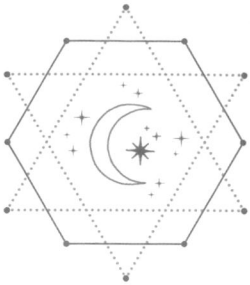

GOALS ALIGNED WITH MY PURPOSE:

ACTION STEPS I CAN TAKE TODAY:

- ☐
- ☐
- ☐
- ☐
- ☐
- ☐

A SELF-CARE GOAL FOR TODAY:

A CHALLENGE I'M FACING:

SOMETHING I'M EXCITED ABOUT:

HOW I SPENT MY TIME TODAY:

- ☐ MY LIFE'S PASSION
- ☐ VOLUNTEERING
- ☐ ONLINE/SOCIAL MEDIA
- ☐ WORKING
- ☐ SELF-CARE
- ☐ DOWN TIME
- ☐ TIME WITH FRIENDS/FAMILY
- ☐ TIME OUTDOORS
- ☐ OTHER: _____

EVENING REFLECTION

HOW I'M FEELING:

THIS BROUGHT ME THE GREATEST JOY TODAY:

SOMETHING I DID TODAY THAT FELT MEANINGFUL:

WHAT I DID TODAY THAT ALIGNED WITH MY PURPOSE:

A NOTABLE RESULT FROM LIVING MY PURPOSE:

A SETBACK I FACED TODAY AND HOW I CAN LEARN OR GROW FROM THIS:

MORNING REFLECTION

DATE ___/___/___

MY PURPOSE OR INTENTION FOR TODAY:

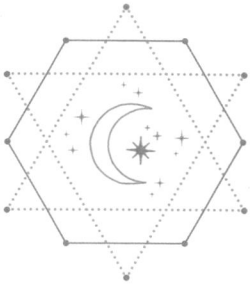

GOALS ALIGNED WITH MY PURPOSE:

ACTION STEPS I CAN TAKE TODAY:

- ☐
- ☐
- ☐
- ☐
- ☐
- ☐

A SELF-CARE GOAL FOR TODAY:

A CHALLENGE I'M FACING:

SOMETHING I'M EXCITED ABOUT:

HOW I SPENT MY TIME TODAY:

- ☐ MY LIFE'S PASSION
- ☐ VOLUNTEERING
- ☐ ONLINE/SOCIAL MEDIA
- ☐ WORKING
- ☐ SELF-CARE
- ☐ DOWN TIME
- ☐ TIME WITH FRIENDS/FAMILY
- ☐ TIME OUTDOORS
- ☐ OTHER: _____

EVENING REFLECTION

HOW I'M FEELING:

THIS BROUGHT ME THE GREATEST JOY TODAY:

SOMETHING I DID TODAY THAT FELT MEANINGFUL:

WHAT I DID TODAY THAT ALIGNED WITH MY PURPOSE:

A NOTABLE RESULT FROM LIVING MY PURPOSE:

A SETBACK I FACED TODAY AND HOW I CAN LEARN OR GROW FROM THIS:

MORNING REFLECTION

DATE ___/___/___

MY PURPOSE OR INTENTION FOR TODAY:

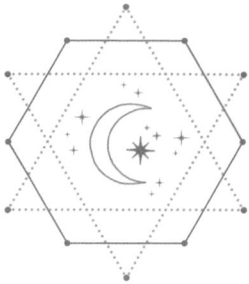

GOALS ALIGNED WITH MY PURPOSE:

ACTION STEPS I CAN TAKE TODAY:

- ☐
- ☐
- ☐
- ☐
- ☐
- ☐

A SELF-CARE GOAL FOR TODAY:

A CHALLENGE I'M FACING:

SOMETHING I'M EXCITED ABOUT:

HOW I SPENT MY TIME TODAY:

- ☐ MY LIFE'S PASSION
- ☐ VOLUNTEERING
- ☐ ONLINE/SOCIAL MEDIA
- ☐ WORKING
- ☐ SELF-CARE
- ☐ DOWN TIME
- ☐ TIME WITH FRIENDS/FAMILY
- ☐ TIME OUTDOORS
- ☐ OTHER: _____

EVENING REFLECTION

HOW I'M FEELING:

THIS BROUGHT ME THE GREATEST JOY TODAY:

SOMETHING I DID TODAY THAT FELT MEANINGFUL:

WHAT I DID TODAY THAT ALIGNED WITH MY PURPOSE:

A NOTABLE RESULT FROM LIVING MY PURPOSE:

A SETBACK I FACED TODAY AND HOW I CAN LEARN OR GROW FROM THIS:

MORNING REFLECTION

DATE ___/___/___

MY PURPOSE OR INTENTION FOR TODAY:

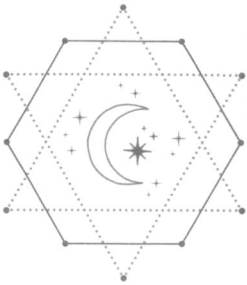

GOALS ALIGNED WITH MY PURPOSE:

ACTION STEPS I CAN TAKE TODAY:

- ☐
- ☐
- ☐
- ☐
- ☐
- ☐

A SELF-CARE GOAL FOR TODAY:

A CHALLENGE I'M FACING:

SOMETHING I'M EXCITED ABOUT:

HOW I SPENT MY TIME TODAY:

- ☐ MY LIFE'S PASSION
- ☐ VOLUNTEERING
- ☐ ONLINE/SOCIAL MEDIA
- ☐ WORKING
- ☐ SELF-CARE
- ☐ DOWN TIME
- ☐ TIME WITH FRIENDS/FAMILY
- ☐ TIME OUTDOORS
- ☐ OTHER: _____

EVENING REFLECTION

HOW I'M FEELING:

THIS BROUGHT ME THE GREATEST JOY TODAY:

SOMETHING I DID TODAY THAT FELT MEANINGFUL:

WHAT I DID TODAY THAT ALIGNED WITH MY PURPOSE:

A NOTABLE RESULT FROM LIVING MY PURPOSE:

A SETBACK I FACED TODAY AND HOW I CAN LEARN OR GROW FROM THIS:

MORNING REFLECTION

DATE ___/___/___

MY PURPOSE OR INTENTION FOR TODAY:

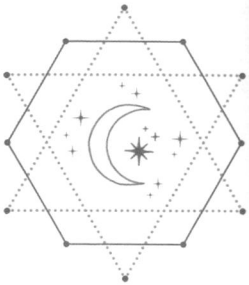

GOALS ALIGNED WITH MY PURPOSE:

ACTION STEPS I CAN TAKE TODAY:

- ☐
- ☐
- ☐
- ☐
- ☐
- ☐

A SELF-CARE GOAL FOR TODAY:

A CHALLENGE I'M FACING:

SOMETHING I'M EXCITED ABOUT:

HOW I SPENT MY TIME TODAY:

- ☐ MY LIFE'S PASSION
- ☐ VOLUNTEERING
- ☐ ONLINE/SOCIAL MEDIA
- ☐ WORKING
- ☐ SELF-CARE
- ☐ DOWN TIME
- ☐ TIME WITH FRIENDS/FAMILY
- ☐ TIME OUTDOORS
- ☐ OTHER: _____

EVENING REFLECTION

HOW I'M FEELING:

THIS BROUGHT ME THE GREATEST JOY TODAY:

SOMETHING I DID TODAY THAT FELT MEANINGFUL:

WHAT I DID TODAY THAT ALIGNED WITH MY PURPOSE:

A NOTABLE RESULT FROM LIVING MY PURPOSE:

A SETBACK I FACED TODAY AND HOW I CAN LEARN OR GROW FROM THIS:

MORNING REFLECTION

DATE ___/___/___

MY PURPOSE OR INTENTION FOR TODAY:

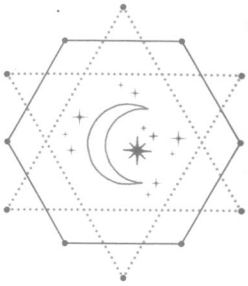

GOALS ALIGNED WITH MY PURPOSE:

ACTION STEPS I CAN TAKE TODAY:

- ☐
- ☐
- ☐
- ☐
- ☐
- ☐

A SELF-CARE GOAL FOR TODAY:

A CHALLENGE I'M FACING:

SOMETHING I'M EXCITED ABOUT:

HOW I SPENT MY TIME TODAY:

- ☐ MY LIFE'S PASSION
- ☐ VOLUNTEERING
- ☐ ONLINE/SOCIAL MEDIA
- ☐ WORKING
- ☐ SELF-CARE
- ☐ DOWN TIME
- ☐ TIME WITH FRIENDS/FAMILY
- ☐ TIME OUTDOORS
- ☐ OTHER: _____

EVENING REFLECTION

HOW I'M FEELING:

THIS BROUGHT ME THE GREATEST JOY TODAY:

SOMETHING I DID TODAY THAT FELT MEANINGFUL:

WHAT I DID TODAY THAT ALIGNED WITH MY PURPOSE:

A NOTABLE RESULT FROM LIVING MY PURPOSE:

A SETBACK I FACED TODAY AND HOW I CAN LEARN OR GROW FROM THIS:

MORNING REFLECTION

DATE ___/___/___

MY PURPOSE OR INTENTION FOR TODAY:

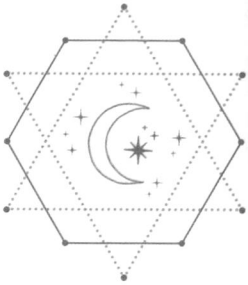

GOALS ALIGNED WITH MY PURPOSE:

ACTION STEPS I CAN TAKE TODAY:

- ☐
- ☐
- ☐
- ☐
- ☐
- ☐

A SELF-CARE GOAL FOR TODAY:

A CHALLENGE I'M FACING:

SOMETHING I'M EXCITED ABOUT:

HOW I SPENT MY TIME TODAY:

- ☐ MY LIFE'S PASSION
- ☐ VOLUNTEERING
- ☐ ONLINE/SOCIAL MEDIA
- ☐ WORKING
- ☐ SELF-CARE
- ☐ DOWN TIME
- ☐ TIME WITH FRIENDS/FAMILY
- ☐ TIME OUTDOORS
- ☐ OTHER: _____

EVENING REFLECTION

HOW I'M FEELING:

THIS BROUGHT ME THE GREATEST JOY TODAY:

SOMETHING I DID TODAY THAT FELT MEANINGFUL:

WHAT I DID TODAY THAT ALIGNED WITH MY PURPOSE:

A NOTABLE RESULT FROM LIVING MY PURPOSE:

A SETBACK I FACED TODAY AND HOW I CAN LEARN OR GROW FROM THIS:

MORNING REFLECTION

DATE ___/___/___

MY PURPOSE OR INTENTION FOR TODAY:

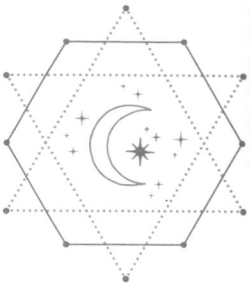

GOALS ALIGNED WITH MY PURPOSE:

ACTION STEPS I CAN TAKE TODAY:

- ☐
- ☐
- ☐
- ☐
- ☐
- ☐

A SELF-CARE GOAL FOR TODAY:

A CHALLENGE I'M FACING:

SOMETHING I'M EXCITED ABOUT:

HOW I SPENT MY TIME TODAY:

- ☐ MY LIFE'S PASSION
- ☐ VOLUNTEERING
- ☐ ONLINE/SOCIAL MEDIA
- ☐ WORKING
- ☐ SELF-CARE
- ☐ DOWN TIME
- ☐ TIME WITH FRIENDS/FAMILY
- ☐ TIME OUTDOORS
- ☐ OTHER: _____

EVENING REFLECTION

HOW I'M FEELING:

THIS BROUGHT ME THE GREATEST JOY TODAY:

SOMETHING I DID TODAY THAT FELT MEANINGFUL:

WHAT I DID TODAY THAT ALIGNED WITH MY PURPOSE:

A NOTABLE RESULT FROM LIVING MY PURPOSE:

A SETBACK I FACED TODAY AND HOW I CAN LEARN OR GROW FROM THIS:

MORNING REFLECTION

DATE ___/___/___

MY PURPOSE OR INTENTION FOR TODAY:

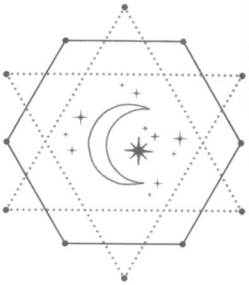

GOALS ALIGNED WITH MY PURPOSE:

ACTION STEPS I CAN TAKE TODAY:

- ☐
- ☐
- ☐
- ☐
- ☐
- ☐

A SELF-CARE GOAL FOR TODAY:

A CHALLENGE I'M FACING:

SOMETHING I'M EXCITED ABOUT:

HOW I SPENT MY TIME TODAY:

- ☐ MY LIFE'S PASSION
- ☐ VOLUNTEERING
- ☐ ONLINE/SOCIAL MEDIA
- ☐ WORKING
- ☐ SELF-CARE
- ☐ DOWN TIME
- ☐ TIME WITH FRIENDS/FAMILY
- ☐ TIME OUTDOORS
- ☐ OTHER: _____

EVENING REFLECTION

HOW I'M FEELING:

THIS BROUGHT ME THE GREATEST JOY TODAY:

SOMETHING I DID TODAY THAT FELT MEANINGFUL:

WHAT I DID TODAY THAT ALIGNED WITH MY PURPOSE:

A NOTABLE RESULT FROM LIVING MY PURPOSE:

A SETBACK I FACED TODAY AND HOW I CAN LEARN OR GROW FROM THIS:

MORNING REFLECTION

DATE ___/___/___

MY PURPOSE OR INTENTION FOR TODAY:

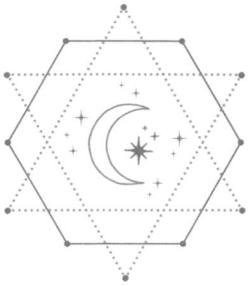

GOALS ALIGNED WITH MY PURPOSE:

ACTION STEPS I CAN TAKE TODAY:

- ☐
- ☐
- ☐
- ☐
- ☐
- ☐

A SELF-CARE GOAL FOR TODAY:

A CHALLENGE I'M FACING:

SOMETHING I'M EXCITED ABOUT:

HOW I SPENT MY TIME TODAY:

- ☐ MY LIFE'S PASSION
- ☐ VOLUNTEERING
- ☐ ONLINE/SOCIAL MEDIA
- ☐ WORKING
- ☐ SELF-CARE
- ☐ DOWN TIME
- ☐ TIME WITH FRIENDS/FAMILY
- ☐ TIME OUTDOORS
- ☐ OTHER: _____

EVENING REFLECTION

HOW I'M FEELING:

THIS BROUGHT ME THE GREATEST JOY TODAY:

SOMETHING I DID TODAY THAT FELT MEANINGFUL:

WHAT I DID TODAY THAT ALIGNED WITH MY PURPOSE:

A NOTABLE RESULT FROM LIVING MY PURPOSE:

A SETBACK I FACED TODAY AND HOW I CAN LEARN OR GROW FROM THIS:

MORNING REFLECTION

DATE ___/___/___

MY PURPOSE OR INTENTION FOR TODAY:

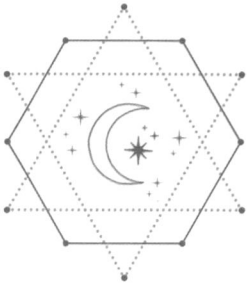

GOALS ALIGNED WITH MY PURPOSE:

ACTION STEPS I CAN TAKE TODAY:

- ☐
- ☐
- ☐
- ☐
- ☐
- ☐

A SELF-CARE GOAL FOR TODAY:

A CHALLENGE I'M FACING:

SOMETHING I'M EXCITED ABOUT:

HOW I SPENT MY TIME TODAY:

- ☐ MY LIFE'S PASSION
- ☐ VOLUNTEERING
- ☐ ONLINE/SOCIAL MEDIA
- ☐ WORKING
- ☐ SELF-CARE
- ☐ DOWN TIME
- ☐ TIME WITH FRIENDS/FAMILY
- ☐ TIME OUTDOORS
- ☐ OTHER: _____

EVENING REFLECTION

HOW I'M FEELING:

THIS BROUGHT ME THE GREATEST JOY TODAY:

SOMETHING I DID TODAY THAT FELT MEANINGFUL:

WHAT I DID TODAY THAT ALIGNED WITH MY PURPOSE:

A NOTABLE RESULT FROM LIVING MY PURPOSE:

A SETBACK I FACED TODAY AND HOW I CAN LEARN OR GROW FROM THIS:

MORNING REFLECTION

DATE ___/___/___

MY PURPOSE OR INTENTION FOR TODAY:

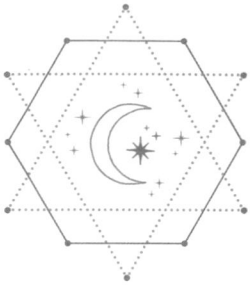

GOALS ALIGNED WITH MY PURPOSE:

ACTION STEPS I CAN TAKE TODAY:

- ☐
- ☐
- ☐
- ☐
- ☐
- ☐

A SELF-CARE GOAL FOR TODAY:

A CHALLENGE I'M FACING:

SOMETHING I'M EXCITED ABOUT:

HOW I SPENT MY TIME TODAY:

- ☐ MY LIFE'S PASSION
- ☐ VOLUNTEERING
- ☐ ONLINE/SOCIAL MEDIA
- ☐ WORKING
- ☐ SELF-CARE
- ☐ DOWN TIME
- ☐ TIME WITH FRIENDS/FAMILY
- ☐ TIME OUTDOORS
- ☐ OTHER: _____

EVENING REFLECTION

HOW I'M FEELING:

THIS BROUGHT ME THE GREATEST JOY TODAY:

SOMETHING I DID TODAY THAT FELT MEANINGFUL:

WHAT I DID TODAY THAT ALIGNED WITH MY PURPOSE:

A NOTABLE RESULT FROM LIVING MY PURPOSE:

A SETBACK I FACED TODAY AND HOW I CAN LEARN OR GROW FROM THIS:

MORNING REFLECTION

DATE ___/___/___

MY PURPOSE OR INTENTION FOR TODAY:

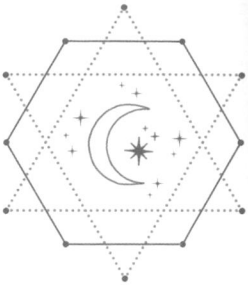

GOALS ALIGNED WITH MY PURPOSE:

ACTION STEPS I CAN TAKE TODAY:

- ☐
- ☐
- ☐
- ☐
- ☐
- ☐

A SELF-CARE GOAL FOR TODAY:

A CHALLENGE I'M FACING:

SOMETHING I'M EXCITED ABOUT:

HOW I SPENT MY TIME TODAY:

- ☐ MY LIFE'S PASSION
- ☐ VOLUNTEERING
- ☐ ONLINE/SOCIAL MEDIA
- ☐ WORKING
- ☐ SELF-CARE
- ☐ DOWN TIME
- ☐ TIME WITH FRIENDS/FAMILY
- ☐ TIME OUTDOORS
- ☐ OTHER: _____

EVENING REFLECTION

HOW I'M FEELING:

THIS BROUGHT ME THE GREATEST JOY TODAY:

SOMETHING I DID TODAY THAT FELT MEANINGFUL:

WHAT I DID TODAY THAT ALIGNED WITH MY PURPOSE:

A NOTABLE RESULT FROM LIVING MY PURPOSE:

A SETBACK I FACED TODAY AND HOW I CAN LEARN OR GROW FROM THIS:

MORNING REFLECTION

DATE ___/___/___

MY PURPOSE OR INTENTION FOR TODAY:

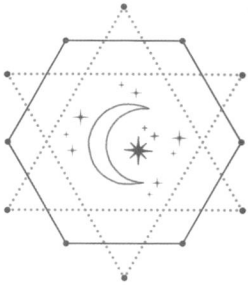

GOALS ALIGNED WITH MY PURPOSE:

ACTION STEPS I CAN TAKE TODAY:

- ☐
- ☐
- ☐
- ☐
- ☐
- ☐

A SELF-CARE GOAL FOR TODAY:

A CHALLENGE I'M FACING:

SOMETHING I'M EXCITED ABOUT:

HOW I SPENT MY TIME TODAY:

- ☐ MY LIFE'S PASSION
- ☐ VOLUNTEERING
- ☐ ONLINE/SOCIAL MEDIA
- ☐ WORKING
- ☐ SELF-CARE
- ☐ DOWN TIME
- ☐ TIME WITH FRIENDS/FAMILY
- ☐ TIME OUTDOORS
- ☐ OTHER: _____

EVENING REFLECTION

HOW I'M FEELING:

THIS BROUGHT ME THE GREATEST JOY TODAY:

SOMETHING I DID TODAY THAT FELT MEANINGFUL:

WHAT I DID TODAY THAT ALIGNED WITH MY PURPOSE:

A NOTABLE RESULT FROM LIVING MY PURPOSE:

A SETBACK I FACED TODAY AND HOW I CAN LEARN OR GROW FROM THIS:

MORNING REFLECTION

DATE ___/___/___

MY PURPOSE OR INTENTION FOR TODAY:

GOALS ALIGNED WITH MY PURPOSE:

ACTION STEPS I CAN TAKE TODAY:

- ☐
- ☐
- ☐
- ☐
- ☐
- ☐

A SELF-CARE GOAL FOR TODAY:

A CHALLENGE I'M FACING:

SOMETHING I'M EXCITED ABOUT:

HOW I SPENT MY TIME TODAY:

- ☐ MY LIFE'S PASSION
- ☐ VOLUNTEERING
- ☐ ONLINE/SOCIAL MEDIA
- ☐ WORKING
- ☐ SELF-CARE
- ☐ DOWN TIME
- ☐ TIME WITH FRIENDS/FAMILY
- ☐ TIME OUTDOORS
- ☐ OTHER: _____

EVENING REFLECTION

HOW I'M FEELING:

THIS BROUGHT ME THE GREATEST JOY TODAY:

SOMETHING I DID TODAY THAT FELT MEANINGFUL:

WHAT I DID TODAY THAT ALIGNED WITH MY PURPOSE:

A NOTABLE RESULT FROM LIVING MY PURPOSE:

A SETBACK I FACED TODAY AND HOW I CAN LEARN OR GROW FROM THIS:

MORNING REFLECTION

DATE ___/___/___

MY PURPOSE OR INTENTION FOR TODAY:

GOALS ALIGNED WITH MY PURPOSE:

ACTION STEPS I CAN TAKE TODAY:

- ☐
- ☐
- ☐
- ☐
- ☐
- ☐

A SELF-CARE GOAL FOR TODAY:

A CHALLENGE I'M FACING:

SOMETHING I'M EXCITED ABOUT:

HOW I SPENT MY TIME TODAY:

- ☐ MY LIFE'S PASSION
- ☐ VOLUNTEERING
- ☐ ONLINE/SOCIAL MEDIA
- ☐ WORKING
- ☐ SELF-CARE
- ☐ DOWN TIME
- ☐ TIME WITH FRIENDS/FAMILY
- ☐ TIME OUTDOORS
- ☐ OTHER: _____

EVENING REFLECTION

HOW I'M FEELING:

THIS BROUGHT ME THE GREATEST JOY TODAY:

SOMETHING I DID TODAY THAT FELT MEANINGFUL:

WHAT I DID TODAY THAT ALIGNED WITH MY PURPOSE:

A NOTABLE RESULT FROM LIVING MY PURPOSE:

A SETBACK I FACED TODAY AND HOW I CAN LEARN OR GROW FROM THIS:

MORNING REFLECTION

DATE ___/___/___

MY PURPOSE OR INTENTION FOR TODAY:

GOALS ALIGNED WITH MY PURPOSE:

ACTION STEPS I CAN TAKE TODAY:

- ☐
- ☐
- ☐
- ☐
- ☐
- ☐

A SELF-CARE GOAL FOR TODAY:

A CHALLENGE I'M FACING:

SOMETHING I'M EXCITED ABOUT:

HOW I SPENT MY TIME TODAY:

- ☐ MY LIFE'S PASSION
- ☐ VOLUNTEERING
- ☐ ONLINE/SOCIAL MEDIA
- ☐ WORKING
- ☐ SELF-CARE
- ☐ DOWN TIME
- ☐ TIME WITH FRIENDS/FAMILY
- ☐ TIME OUTDOORS
- ☐ OTHER: _____

EVENING REFLECTION

HOW I'M FEELING:

THIS BROUGHT ME THE GREATEST JOY TODAY:

SOMETHING I DID TODAY THAT FELT MEANINGFUL:

WHAT I DID TODAY THAT ALIGNED WITH MY PURPOSE:

A NOTABLE RESULT FROM LIVING MY PURPOSE:

A SETBACK I FACED TODAY AND HOW I CAN LEARN OR GROW FROM THIS:

MORNING REFLECTION

DATE ___/___/___

MY PURPOSE OR INTENTION FOR TODAY:

GOALS ALIGNED WITH MY PURPOSE:

ACTION STEPS I CAN TAKE TODAY:

- ☐
- ☐
- ☐
- ☐
- ☐
- ☐

A SELF-CARE GOAL FOR TODAY:

A CHALLENGE I'M FACING:

SOMETHING I'M EXCITED ABOUT:

HOW I SPENT MY TIME TODAY:

- ☐ MY LIFE'S PASSION
- ☐ VOLUNTEERING
- ☐ ONLINE/SOCIAL MEDIA
- ☐ WORKING
- ☐ SELF-CARE
- ☐ DOWN TIME
- ☐ TIME WITH FRIENDS/FAMILY
- ☐ TIME OUTDOORS
- ☐ OTHER: _____

EVENING REFLECTION

HOW I'M FEELING:

THIS BROUGHT ME THE GREATEST JOY TODAY:

SOMETHING I DID TODAY THAT FELT MEANINGFUL:

WHAT I DID TODAY THAT ALIGNED WITH MY PURPOSE:

A NOTABLE RESULT FROM LIVING MY PURPOSE:

A SETBACK I FACED TODAY AND HOW I CAN LEARN OR GROW FROM THIS:

MORNING REFLECTION

DATE ___/___/___

MY PURPOSE OR INTENTION FOR TODAY:

GOALS ALIGNED WITH MY PURPOSE:

ACTION STEPS I CAN TAKE TODAY:

- ☐
- ☐
- ☐
- ☐
- ☐
- ☐

A SELF-CARE GOAL FOR TODAY:

A CHALLENGE I'M FACING:

SOMETHING I'M EXCITED ABOUT:

HOW I SPENT MY TIME TODAY:

- ☐ MY LIFE'S PASSION
- ☐ WORKING
- ☐ TIME WITH FRIENDS/FAMILY
- ☐ VOLUNTEERING
- ☐ SELF-CARE
- ☐ TIME OUTDOORS
- ☐ ONLINE/SOCIAL MEDIA
- ☐ DOWN TIME
- ☐ OTHER: _____

EVENING REFLECTION

HOW I'M FEELING:

THIS BROUGHT ME THE GREATEST JOY TODAY:

SOMETHING I DID TODAY THAT FELT MEANINGFUL:

WHAT I DID TODAY THAT ALIGNED WITH MY PURPOSE:

A NOTABLE RESULT FROM LIVING MY PURPOSE:

A SETBACK I FACED TODAY AND HOW I CAN LEARN OR GROW FROM THIS:

MORNING REFLECTION

DATE ___/___/___

MY PURPOSE OR INTENTION FOR TODAY:

GOALS ALIGNED WITH MY PURPOSE:

ACTION STEPS I CAN TAKE TODAY:

- ☐
- ☐
- ☐
- ☐
- ☐
- ☐

A SELF-CARE GOAL FOR TODAY:

A CHALLENGE I'M FACING:

SOMETHING I'M EXCITED ABOUT:

HOW I SPENT MY TIME TODAY:

- ☐ MY LIFE'S PASSION
- ☐ VOLUNTEERING
- ☐ ONLINE/SOCIAL MEDIA
- ☐ WORKING
- ☐ SELF-CARE
- ☐ DOWN TIME
- ☐ TIME WITH FRIENDS/FAMILY
- ☐ TIME OUTDOORS
- ☐ OTHER: _____

EVENING REFLECTION

HOW I'M FEELING:

THIS BROUGHT ME THE GREATEST JOY TODAY:

SOMETHING I DID TODAY THAT FELT MEANINGFUL:

WHAT I DID TODAY THAT ALIGNED WITH MY PURPOSE:

A NOTABLE RESULT FROM LIVING MY PURPOSE:

A SETBACK I FACED TODAY AND HOW I CAN LEARN OR GROW FROM THIS:

MORNING REFLECTION

DATE ___/___/___

MY PURPOSE OR INTENTION FOR TODAY:

GOALS ALIGNED WITH MY PURPOSE:

ACTION STEPS I CAN TAKE TODAY:

- ☐
- ☐
- ☐
- ☐
- ☐
- ☐

A SELF-CARE GOAL FOR TODAY:

A CHALLENGE I'M FACING:

SOMETHING I'M EXCITED ABOUT:

HOW I SPENT MY TIME TODAY:

- ☐ MY LIFE'S PASSION
- ☐ VOLUNTEERING
- ☐ ONLINE/SOCIAL MEDIA
- ☐ WORKING
- ☐ SELF-CARE
- ☐ DOWN TIME
- ☐ TIME WITH FRIENDS/FAMILY
- ☐ TIME OUTDOORS
- ☐ OTHER: _____

EVENING REFLECTION

HOW I'M FEELING:

THIS BROUGHT ME THE GREATEST JOY TODAY:

SOMETHING I DID TODAY THAT FELT MEANINGFUL:

WHAT I DID TODAY THAT ALIGNED WITH MY PURPOSE:

A NOTABLE RESULT FROM LIVING MY PURPOSE:

A SETBACK I FACED TODAY AND HOW I CAN LEARN OR GROW FROM THIS:

MORNING REFLECTION

DATE ___/___/___

MY PURPOSE OR INTENTION FOR TODAY:

GOALS ALIGNED WITH MY PURPOSE:

ACTION STEPS I CAN TAKE TODAY:

- ☐
- ☐
- ☐
- ☐
- ☐
- ☐

A SELF-CARE GOAL FOR TODAY:

A CHALLENGE I'M FACING:

SOMETHING I'M EXCITED ABOUT:

HOW I SPENT MY TIME TODAY:

- ☐ MY LIFE'S PASSION
- ☐ VOLUNTEERING
- ☐ ONLINE/SOCIAL MEDIA
- ☐ WORKING
- ☐ SELF-CARE
- ☐ DOWN TIME
- ☐ TIME WITH FRIENDS/FAMILY
- ☐ TIME OUTDOORS
- ☐ OTHER: _____

EVENING REFLECTION

HOW I'M FEELING:

THIS BROUGHT ME THE GREATEST JOY TODAY:

SOMETHING I DID TODAY THAT FELT MEANINGFUL:

WHAT I DID TODAY THAT ALIGNED WITH MY PURPOSE:

A NOTABLE RESULT FROM LIVING MY PURPOSE:

A SETBACK I FACED TODAY AND HOW I CAN LEARN OR GROW FROM THIS:

MORNING REFLECTION

DATE ___/___/___

MY PURPOSE OR INTENTION FOR TODAY:

GOALS ALIGNED WITH MY PURPOSE:

ACTION STEPS I CAN TAKE TODAY:

- ☐
- ☐
- ☐
- ☐
- ☐
- ☐

A SELF-CARE GOAL FOR TODAY:

A CHALLENGE I'M FACING:

SOMETHING I'M EXCITED ABOUT:

HOW I SPENT MY TIME TODAY:

- ☐ MY LIFE'S PASSION
- ☐ VOLUNTEERING
- ☐ ONLINE/SOCIAL MEDIA
- ☐ WORKING
- ☐ SELF-CARE
- ☐ DOWN TIME
- ☐ TIME WITH FRIENDS/FAMILY
- ☐ TIME OUTDOORS
- ☐ OTHER: _____

EVENING REFLECTION

HOW I'M FEELING:

THIS BROUGHT ME THE GREATEST JOY TODAY:

SOMETHING I DID TODAY THAT FELT MEANINGFUL:

WHAT I DID TODAY THAT ALIGNED WITH MY PURPOSE:

A NOTABLE RESULT FROM LIVING MY PURPOSE:

A SETBACK I FACED TODAY AND HOW I CAN LEARN OR GROW FROM THIS:

MORNING REFLECTION

DATE ___/___/___

MY PURPOSE OR INTENTION FOR TODAY:

GOALS ALIGNED WITH MY PURPOSE:

ACTION STEPS I CAN TAKE TODAY:

- ☐
- ☐
- ☐
- ☐
- ☐
- ☐

A SELF-CARE GOAL FOR TODAY:

A CHALLENGE I'M FACING:

SOMETHING I'M EXCITED ABOUT:

HOW I SPENT MY TIME TODAY:

- ☐ MY LIFE'S PASSION
- ☐ VOLUNTEERING
- ☐ ONLINE/SOCIAL MEDIA
- ☐ WORKING
- ☐ SELF-CARE
- ☐ DOWN TIME
- ☐ TIME WITH FRIENDS/FAMILY
- ☐ TIME OUTDOORS
- ☐ OTHER: _____

EVENING REFLECTION

HOW I'M FEELING:

THIS BROUGHT ME THE GREATEST JOY TODAY:

SOMETHING I DID TODAY THAT FELT MEANINGFUL:

WHAT I DID TODAY THAT ALIGNED WITH MY PURPOSE:

A NOTABLE RESULT FROM LIVING MY PURPOSE:

A SETBACK I FACED TODAY AND HOW I CAN LEARN OR GROW FROM THIS:

MORNING REFLECTION

DATE ___/___/___

MY PURPOSE OR INTENTION FOR TODAY:

GOALS ALIGNED WITH MY PURPOSE:

ACTION STEPS I CAN TAKE TODAY:

- ☐
- ☐
- ☐
- ☐
- ☐
- ☐

A SELF-CARE GOAL FOR TODAY:

A CHALLENGE I'M FACING:

SOMETHING I'M EXCITED ABOUT:

HOW I SPENT MY TIME TODAY:

- ☐ MY LIFE'S PASSION
- ☐ VOLUNTEERING
- ☐ ONLINE/SOCIAL MEDIA
- ☐ WORKING
- ☐ SELF-CARE
- ☐ DOWN TIME
- ☐ TIME WITH FRIENDS/FAMILY
- ☐ TIME OUTDOORS
- ☐ OTHER: _____

EVENING REFLECTION

HOW I'M FEELING:

THIS BROUGHT ME THE GREATEST JOY TODAY:

SOMETHING I DID TODAY THAT FELT MEANINGFUL:

WHAT I DID TODAY THAT ALIGNED WITH MY PURPOSE:

A NOTABLE RESULT FROM LIVING MY PURPOSE:

A SETBACK I FACED TODAY AND HOW I CAN LEARN OR GROW FROM THIS:

MORNING REFLECTION

DATE ___/___/___

MY PURPOSE OR INTENTION FOR TODAY:

GOALS ALIGNED WITH MY PURPOSE:

ACTION STEPS I CAN TAKE TODAY:

- ☐
- ☐
- ☐
- ☐
- ☐
- ☐

A SELF-CARE GOAL FOR TODAY:

A CHALLENGE I'M FACING:

SOMETHING I'M EXCITED ABOUT:

HOW I SPENT MY TIME TODAY:

- ☐ MY LIFE'S PASSION
- ☐ VOLUNTEERING
- ☐ ONLINE/SOCIAL MEDIA
- ☐ WORKING
- ☐ SELF-CARE
- ☐ DOWN TIME
- ☐ TIME WITH FRIENDS/FAMILY
- ☐ TIME OUTDOORS
- ☐ OTHER: _____

EVENING REFLECTION

HOW I'M FEELING:

THIS BROUGHT ME THE GREATEST JOY TODAY:

SOMETHING I DID TODAY THAT FELT MEANINGFUL:

WHAT I DID TODAY THAT ALIGNED WITH MY PURPOSE:

A NOTABLE RESULT FROM LIVING MY PURPOSE:

A SETBACK I FACED TODAY AND HOW I CAN LEARN OR GROW FROM THIS:

MORNING REFLECTION

DATE ___/___/___

MY PURPOSE OR INTENTION FOR TODAY:

GOALS ALIGNED WITH MY PURPOSE:

ACTION STEPS I CAN TAKE TODAY:

- ☐
- ☐
- ☐
- ☐
- ☐
- ☐

A SELF-CARE GOAL FOR TODAY:

A CHALLENGE I'M FACING:

SOMETHING I'M EXCITED ABOUT:

HOW I SPENT MY TIME TODAY:

- ☐ MY LIFE'S PASSION
- ☐ VOLUNTEERING
- ☐ ONLINE/SOCIAL MEDIA
- ☐ WORKING
- ☐ SELF-CARE
- ☐ DOWN TIME
- ☐ TIME WITH FRIENDS/FAMILY
- ☐ TIME OUTDOORS
- ☐ OTHER: _____

EVENING REFLECTION

HOW I'M FEELING:

THIS BROUGHT ME THE GREATEST JOY TODAY:

SOMETHING I DID TODAY THAT FELT MEANINGFUL:

WHAT I DID TODAY THAT ALIGNED WITH MY PURPOSE:

A NOTABLE RESULT FROM LIVING MY PURPOSE:

A SETBACK I FACED TODAY AND HOW I CAN LEARN OR GROW FROM THIS:

MORNING REFLECTION

DATE ___/___/___

MY PURPOSE OR INTENTION FOR TODAY:

GOALS ALIGNED WITH MY PURPOSE:

ACTION STEPS I CAN TAKE TODAY:

- ☐
- ☐
- ☐
- ☐
- ☐
- ☐

A SELF-CARE GOAL FOR TODAY:

A CHALLENGE I'M FACING:

SOMETHING I'M EXCITED ABOUT:

HOW I SPENT MY TIME TODAY:

- ☐ MY LIFE'S PASSION
- ☐ VOLUNTEERING
- ☐ ONLINE/SOCIAL MEDIA
- ☐ WORKING
- ☐ SELF-CARE
- ☐ DOWN TIME
- ☐ TIME WITH FRIENDS/FAMILY
- ☐ TIME OUTDOORS
- ☐ OTHER: _____

EVENING REFLECTION

HOW I'M FEELING:

THIS BROUGHT ME THE GREATEST JOY TODAY:

SOMETHING I DID TODAY THAT FELT MEANINGFUL:

WHAT I DID TODAY THAT ALIGNED WITH MY PURPOSE:

A NOTABLE RESULT FROM LIVING MY PURPOSE:

A SETBACK I FACED TODAY AND HOW I CAN LEARN OR GROW FROM THIS:

MORNING REFLECTION

DATE ___/___/___

MY PURPOSE OR INTENTION FOR TODAY:

GOALS ALIGNED WITH MY PURPOSE:

ACTION STEPS I CAN TAKE TODAY:

- ☐
- ☐
- ☐
- ☐
- ☐
- ☐

A SELF-CARE GOAL FOR TODAY:

A CHALLENGE I'M FACING:

SOMETHING I'M EXCITED ABOUT:

HOW I SPENT MY TIME TODAY:

- ☐ MY LIFE'S PASSION
- ☐ VOLUNTEERING
- ☐ ONLINE/SOCIAL MEDIA
- ☐ WORKING
- ☐ SELF-CARE
- ☐ DOWN TIME
- ☐ TIME WITH FRIENDS/FAMILY
- ☐ TIME OUTDOORS
- ☐ OTHER: _____

EVENING REFLECTION

HOW I'M FEELING:

THIS BROUGHT ME THE GREATEST JOY TODAY:

SOMETHING I DID TODAY THAT FELT MEANINGFUL:

WHAT I DID TODAY THAT ALIGNED WITH MY PURPOSE:

A NOTABLE RESULT FROM LIVING MY PURPOSE:

A SETBACK I FACED TODAY AND HOW I CAN LEARN OR GROW FROM THIS:

INSIGHTS

A Mandala Journal

MANDALA
PUBLISHING

www.mandalaearth.com

Art Direction and Design by Ashley Quackenbush

Copyright © 2023 Mandala Publishing. All rights reserved.

MANUFACTURED IN CHINA

10 9 8 7 6 5 4 3 2 1